# PAYING FORWARD AND GIVING BACK
## *EVERY LIFE HAS PURPOSE*

Deborah A. Vaughn

Author Photo Credit (Back Cover): Troy Alexander

Scripture quotation is taken from THE AMPLIFIED BIBLE, Old Testament copyright ©
1965, 1987 by the Zondervan Corporation. The Amplified New Testament copyright ©
1958, 1987 by the Lockman Foundation. Used by permission

## DEDICATION

To Glen & Fran

and

In loving memory of

Delores Holmes

# TABLE OF CONTENTS

Preface 7

Introduction: Those Who Hear the Call 11

Chapter One: The Final Authority 15

Chapter Two: Accepting the Call 23

Chapter Three: The Chosen Few 31

Chapter Four: You Are the Solution 39

Chapter Five: For the Least of These My Brothers 47

Chapter Six: It's Not About You 55

Chapter Seven: Who Needs You 63

Chapter Eight: Paying Forward 79

Chapter Nine: Giving Back 87

Chapter Ten: Meeting the Challenge 111

Chapter Eleven: Take a Look in the Mirror 121

Chapter Twelve: Obedience Equals Rewards 133

Conclusion: Will You Accept the Call? 141

Musical Suggestions 150

## PREFACE

At the point in my life when I first began to discover my purpose, I was inspired by the things I read in my Bible more than ever before. Growing up in a Christian home, the Bible had always been an integral part of my spiritual training, the final authority on life. However, it seemed to be compartmentalized into a little box marked, "All Things Spiritual", not integrated into the other parts of my life. Moving forward to my adulthood, into a time when my personal challenges greatly outweighed my successes, the passages I read in my Bible became more real and applicable to every aspect of my life.

I was a divorced, single mother with personal, emotional, relationship, and financial struggles. My life was overwhelming and each day brought new battles.

When my eyes opened in the morning from a restless sleep, my feet hit the floor running and my hands were poised for a fight. With three small children strapped to my back, I fought day and night for our survival. My faith in God was my sole source of security, strength and comfort. Somehow in the midst of all of this turmoil, I still found myself seeking success and my life's ultimate purpose.

I knew that God had a plan for me and for my children and the reason for my difficulties and discontent was that I had not been following it. Nothing in my life had worked out the way I had expected it to. It was then that I experienced a spiritual awakening, placing failure and defeat behind me, I looked to my only hope for guidance, which was God. I began to discover revelation and inspiration in everything. From television and billboards to music and my Bible, my knowledge and understanding were continuously nourished. Wisdom had become available to me, I just needed to listen and learn.

I was unemployed and concerned about financially supporting my family. But with greater urgency, I was determined to get in step with God's plan for me. I knew His plan would be the key to changing my reality. With this dual objective I set out to find my way. I felt like my life's plan would include making a difference in the lives of others while taking care of myself. The journey was long from then until now. But, the following book reflects how all the pieces of my existence began to come together. My education, my Bible, my talents, and my passions slowly started to line up with each other and make sense.

This book is an instruction manual that I received in 1998, at the beginning of the difficult process of organizing my existence, discovering my REAL plan, and embarking upon the journey of my lifetime. It helped me gain purpose, perspective and motivation. My hope is that it will do the same for you.

## INTRODUCTION: THOSE WHO HEAR THE CALL

While participating in a charity event with Holiday Express[1] in 2002 at a school for disabled adults, I observed a sign over a doorway that read, "We are not humans on a spiritual journey. We are spirits on a human journey." Simple, but profound. We are spirits who are taking a human journey for a short snippet of time in eternity. During this journey, we are commissioned to complete assignments before we move on to the next phase of our spiritual travel. When we are on track with our assignments, our spirits are fulfilled and peaceful. However, when we are not on track, our spirits are restless and unsatisfied. This is why

---

[1] Holiday Express is a non-sectarian, charitable organization that works year-round to deliver music, food, gifts, and human kindness to adults and children in need.

success (by its common definition) can leave a person empty and searching for satisfaction. Such fulfillment can only be found in your life's purpose.

The fact that you decided to pick up this book probably means that you understand this concept and are seeking to discover and carry out your assignment. You already know that you are meant for something more than what you are doing right now. Somewhere deep inside of you, you can hear the call. You want to understand your calling and get about the business of answering it. You know that your ultimate joy and contentment will be found in doing so.

> We are not humans on a spiritual journey. We are spirits on a human journey.

Do you have an inherent desire to use your talents and resources to help others, to reach out, and to share the wealth? Is life more fulfilling when you are able to give to others? Do you enjoy participating in activities that impact the lives of others in a positive way? Are you somehow not satisfied if you are not making a difference? Then you, like many others, hear the call to service. It is the call to help your fellow man. In all that you do in life, you are called to share your time, talents and resources with others to improve their quality of life. Your assignment is to give and by giving, you enrich your life's journey.

Congratulations! You have been given a truly splendid assignment and are now embarking upon the adventure of a lifetime. You have been hand-selected because of your unique qualities to assist your fellow spirits along this human journey. Such an assignment is an honor, and the rewards greatly outweigh the challenges. As a bonus, an instruction manual has been provided for your assignment. This little book explains the procedures, rules and precautions to making your journey successful and helps you manage mistakes and disappointment.

The instruction manual for your assignment is found in the New Testament of the Holy Bible, in chapter six of the book of Luke. In this chapter, Christ, the great teacher, offers guidance concerning ethics, relationships, rewards, success and submission to the assignment. By reading and internalizing the information in this book, you will gain a greater understanding of your life's purpose. By following its instructions and heeding its warnings, you will increase the probability of your success. By living your assignment, you will greatly enrich your life's journey. There is joy and contentment in serving others, and it is a privilege to those who answer the call in order to experience it.

## CHAPTER ONE: THE FINAL AUTHORITY

Luke 6:1-5

1  *One Sabbath while Jesus was passing through the fields of standing grain, it occurred that His disciples picked some of the spikes and ate [of the grain], rubbing it out in their hands.*

2  *But some of the Pharisees asked them, Why are you doing what is not permitted to be done on the Sabbath days?*

3  *And Jesus replied to them, saying, Have you never so much as read what David did when he was hungry, he and those who were with him?*

4  *How he went into the house of God and took and ate the [sacred] loaves of the showbread, which it is not permitted for any except only the priests to eat, and also gave to those [who were] with him?*

5  *And He said to them, The Son of Man is Lord even of the Sabbath.*

In this passage, some of Jesus' followers stopped to satisfy their hunger with what was readily available to them.  They helped themselves to some of the grain in a field they were passing on their journey. The Pharisees argued that eating the grain was unlawful during the observance of the Sabbath. By picking the grain, rubbing it in their hands and eating it, the Pharisees argued, that they were performing the labor of harvesting and preparing food, both of which was unlawful during the observance of the Sabbath. Using this as a basis, they accused Jesus of encouraging practices that violated rabbinical law.

Upon closer examination, we find that rabbinical law allowed for works of necessity and mercy to be performed on the Sabbath in order to care for one's physical needs. It was normal for people to bathe and feed themselves, or care for their children and livestock on the Sabbath. These kinds of labor were necessary on any day. Although the Pharisees were well aware of this, they spent much of their time devising ways to discredit Jesus, because he was a threat to the status quo.

The Pharisees lived a self-righteous existence, lavishing themselves with luxuries while pointing out the faults of everyone else. It was their practice to feast sumptuously especially on Sabbath days while resting from physical labor. Who was preparing all that food anyway? The Pharisees' accusation was a classic case of pointing out the speck in another's eye while ignoring the log in one's own. The disciples were not violating any rabbinical law. However, their accusers commonly manipulated the law to suit their own wishes.

Jesus, on the other hand, walked among the people. He taught that people should not esteem themselves higher than others, that everyone had short-comings and the focus should be on loving one another. His disciples had merely eaten some raw grain to satisfy hunger and to sustain them on their journey. The law was not meant to cause people to suffer, only for people to set aside time to reverence God. Surely the Pharisees, being well educated in the scriptures, knew this.

Jesus responded to them using an example from the very scriptures on which they based their accusations. He, being the Son of God, took authority over such nonsense, by declaring His Lordship over all things, including the harvest. He asserted Himself as the final authority on what is lawful. Jesus was God in the flesh and the law was established by God. There was no way that Jesus could allow the Pharisees to manipulate God's law and use it against him. He knew his assignment here on earth was to fulfill that very law and no one would keep him from that assignment.

In trying to fulfill your own assignment and placing human service at the forefront of your goals, you may sometimes be accused of inappropriate behavior. Let me explain. With our world in its current state, many are starving, homeless, helpless and neglected. Our political systems are not focused on such people as a priority. Little significance is placed upon helping those who are unable to be productive. The poor, aged, ill, and disabled are considered a social burden. This is why such phenomena as *invisible* homeless people live under the beautiful bridges of our cities. This is why there are *missing* children for whom no one searches. It is the reason that many institutionalized people suffer

*Your work is not bound by political correctness or public opinion.*

powerlessly at the hands of *imaginary* abusers. The real life examples go on and on.

Is it not appalling that while the indigent are surrounded by those of us who enjoy more privilege, few of us can see their tears, hear their screams or feel their pain? You are one of the people who can. To you, social ills do exist and are not invisible. You choose to recognize human need and suffering. It bothers you. But, believe it or not, your compassion may *bother* some people. Your concern for those who are commonly ignored will make some people uncomfortable. Therefore, it is likely that you may encounter opposition to your efforts.

For some, your insistence upon helping the helpless makes them feel guilty. It stirs the conscience and forces us to ask the hard questions. Your concern makes people face themselves. It causes them to reevaluate their responsibility to mankind and that causes different reactions. For some, facing the "Man in the Mirror" causes a positive change and brings about a resetting of priorities. But for those who are not willing to face themselves, it may lead to resentment and you may become the target, because you are the one holding the mirror.

Although you may be accused of showing off, trying to make others look bad, or being a martyr, you must remember this; your calling does not come from people, but from God. Your work is not bound by political correctness or public opinion. It is only driven by God's need to take care of the needy and your willingness to help. So when you decide to serve families at a soup kitchen before sitting down to dinner with your own, it is God in your own heart that you answer to. If you feel the need to teach your child to donate some of her allowance to a poor child in a foreign country, it is not your friend's approval that you seek. You seek only to pass on your deepest convictions to the next generation.

It brings to mind an analogy often told to me by my father when discussing a good work ethic. Born to a poor family at the beginning of the Great Depression, he understood hard work from a young age. As my siblings and I grew up in the 1970s, he talked to us about entering the workforce and always told us to do our best at whatever we might be hired to do. He explained that everyone on a job might not do their best work and by you doing your best, their shortcomings may be brought to light. Dad used to tell us a story of a guy who worked hard on a new job and how he drew resentment from other workers. In the story, the other workers would come to the new worker and tell him to slack off a little because he was doing too much and making them look bad. My Dad would tell us not to concern ourselves with what everyone else was doing. When we are hired to do a job, we should show up on time and do our best work until quitting time. His advice served me well as a young person and even into my professional career. In seeking to put my best foot forward, I usually revealed other talents that were not apparent to my superiors when I was hired. I cannot say that I drew much resentment from colleagues nor was I concerned about it. I just wanted to show that I was worthy of my hire and a good decision on the part of my boss. So without much concern about the amount or quality of other people's work, I just tried to give my best work and that worked out well for me.

God is the Lord over all things. He is the Lord of the harvest and of the food pantry. He calls upon all of us to look out for one another and that is not subject to anyone's approval. So go with God. Follow your calling. Listen to that still, small voice and be your brother's keeper. God is the final authority when you want to know what is right and wrong, proper and improper. Do not concern yourself with popular opinion. It changes with the times. And if others find that your work forces them to deal with their own demons, so be it. We must all live with ourselves and all of us must ultimately answer to God. You have chosen to answer now, to follow your call, and to reach your destiny. The problem with a lot of people is that they fail to see the importance of charity in the realization of their own dreams. Maybe your work will inspire someone to better understand that they need to assume some responsibility for those who are less fortunate in order to reach their own goals.

## CHAPTER TWO:  ACCEPTING THE CALL

Luke 6:6-11

6  *And it occurred on another Sabbath that when He
went into the synagogue and taught, a man was
present whose right hand was withered.*

7  *And the scribes and the Pharisees kept watching
Jesus to see whether He would [actually] heal on the
Sabbath, in order that they might get [some ground
for] accusation against Him.*

8. *But He was aware all along of their thoughts, and He
said to the man with the withered hand, Come and
stand here in the midst.  And he arose and stood
there.*

9  *Then said Jesus to them, I ask you, is it lawful and
right on the Sabbath to do good [so that someone
derives advantage from it] or to do evil, or save life
[and make a soul safe] or to destroy it?*

10  *Then He glanced around at them all and said to the
man, Stretch out your hand! And he did so, and his
hand was fully restored like the other one.*

11  *But they were filled with lack of understanding and
senseless rage and discussed (consulted) with one
another what they might do to Jesus.*

In this example, the Pharisees thought they would set Jesus up in a no-win situation. They wanted to see if he would follow his compassion or try to abide by their interpretation of the law as not to cause a public controversy. However, no matter what he chose to do, their plan was to accuse him. If he helped the man with the withered hand, he would be accused of breaking rabbinical laws concerning the observance of the Sabbath. If he did not help him, he would be accused of hypocrisy, because he had taught people to be compassionate to those in need.

The accusers thought they had him cornered. However, they did not realize that Jesus had little concern about their interpretation of the law and how they traditionally used it to dictate people's actions. His focus was on the fulfillment of his calling. For him, a person in need would always take precedence over people's traditions and opinions. He questioned his accusers openly as to what the law permitted on the Sabbath when it came to helping someone in need. Then, he immediately returned his focus to the man. Knowing that he was doing nothing wrong, Jesus did not hesitate to help the man while everyone observed.

Relieving his suffering was an act of mercy and everyone knew that the law permitted such activities, even on the Sabbath days.

When confronted with traditions and social practices, Jesus chose to engage his accusers out in the open. He called their bluffs based on their own belief system and welcomed their debate on the lawfulness of human kindness. His focus was not on what people would think of him. He had accepted his calling from God and sought to fulfill it at all costs. The accusations that he suffered were accepted as par for the course and he dealt with them as needed. He never allowed such interference to distract him from his work.

When we accept the call to human service, we must do it with a commitment that goes beyond how we measure up to popular opinion. In accepting such a mission, we answer to a higher authority. We understand that while we must abide by laws to maintain order in a civil society, in our commitment to our own purpose, we do not answer to other people or government. We respond to God's leading and inspiration. We obey laws, but do not always follow popular interpretations of them. We do not seek to do harm to anyone, only to do good to those who need our help. We do not avenge against others with whom we do not agree. Our focus is on helping.

When you seek to do good with ultimate sincerity, opposing forces will often be present to accuse you of various infractions. You must not allow such annoyances to interrupt your work. You must deal with accusations when they are unavoidable and stay focused otherwise. However, it is possible that these nuisances can be a positive influence. They can serve as a reminder to always perform your acts of kindness with integrity. You must operate with wisdom and remain blameless in your actions. All of your deeds must be done in the open for all to observe. This subjects you to the criticism of your opposers as well as the praise of your supporters. Nothing that you do needs to be hidden because you are acting upon your divine calling. Even anonymous gifts are somehow reported

> You must operate in wisdom and remain blameless in your actions.

and accounted for. Although your deeds may sometimes annoy your antagonists, their accusations will have little influence on your work.

A few years into my first corporate job after college, I had become pretty comfortable in my work. I had done great work for the company and had been recognized with several promotions and raises. I was accustomed to what were acceptable practices in our office and conducted myself accordingly. Then I was assigned a new project and a new Project Manager to whom I was to report. This manager found a great deal of difficulty in guiding this project in a productive manner and our team spent a lot of time spinning our wheels. I'm sure as the secondary programmer on the project, I could have stepped up and helped out more, but I chose to stick to my own responsibilities and nothing more. Several weeks into the project, it was apparent that the team had been unproductive and the project had been managed poorly. It was at this point that the Project Manager decided to *throw me under the bus* in order to save her own skin. I had followed all of her instructions and handled all of the responsibilities that were delegated to me. However, some common office practices came back to haunt me. Although the things I did were common practice in the office (e.g. personal phone calls, coffee breaks, etc.) these practices were used against me and embellished with lies for effect. She took these common things and documented them as reasons that I had not held up my end of the project. She accused me of doing nothing for weeks. The project had not been moving forward and there was little to show for all the work that I had put into it. I prided myself in being that good worker of whom my Dad would have been proud. This experience was a painful one, but one from which I learned a great life lesson.

I realized that had I held myself to a higher standard in the way I did my job, it would have been more difficult for her to bring accusations against me. Her accusations had a thread of truth that had been woven together in a way to destroy my professional image and position. Her real objective was to divert attention from her own incompetence as a Project Manager and to make me a scapegoat. In all of this, God was merciful to me. I felt like I had sidestepped a bullet when I was able to post out to a different department and a better position before any possible disciplinary action was taken (I don't know that our department management bought her whole story). But in my new position, I worked in a great department, and was rewarded for my talents and hard work. This was a difficult, but valuable lesson for me.

When you seek to follow God's calling in helping others, you engage the opposition and fault finders. People like this do not believe that authentic kindness and goodwill really exist in the world. Often the reason is that their own challenges have caused them to become cynical and callous about life. Their negativity doesn't allow them to see people helped and God glorified. Because of this, some people will be looking for ways and reasons to accuse you. Are you visiting with HIV/AIDS babies because you had abortions earlier in your life? Are you visiting the elderly because you didn't love your own parents? Are you building a community center to increase your position in the community? Is your donation to a homeless shelter just advertisement for your business? Are you a board member for a charity because of financial perks? It really does not matter what accusations may be brought against you as long as all that you do is of the highest integrity. You must be wise, obedient to God's leading and very much blameless in all of your deeds. All of your activities must be above board and open to the scrutiny of any interested party so that there will be no real grounds for the accusations. Let them scrutinize and accuse, you have nothing to fear when your ethics are held to God's standards.

## CHAPTER THREE:  THE CHOSEN FEW

<u>Luke 6:12-16</u>

12  *Now in those days it occurred that He went up into a mountain to pray, and spent the whole night in prayer to God.*

13  *And when it was day, He summoned His disciples and selected from them twelve, whom He named apostles (special messengers):*

14  *They were Simon, whom He named Peter, and his brother Andrew; and James and John, and Philip and Bartholomew;*

15  *And Matthew and Thomas; and James son of Alphaeus, and Simon who was called the Zealot,*

16  *And Judas son of James, and Judas Iscariot, who became a traitor (a treacherous, basely faithless person).*

After prayer and contemplation, Jesus chose from his many followers, twelve whom he would call his special messengers.  These twelve were selected to walk closely with him and to learn from him intimately.

They would be the ones who would receive enlightenment and be able to carry on his legacy long after he was gone. What they were really going to learn is their purpose and assignment here on Earth – to serve their fellow man. They would be taught to follow the inner leading of their own spirit the way Jesus did. They would rise to a higher level of consciousness and live the rest of their experiences helping others to also rise. These twelve special people were put in a precarious position. I'm sure they probably didn't know what to expect or what would be expected of them. But they trusted Jesus enough to answer the call and sign on for the position without question. They would be enlightened to the higher power that worked within them. And in return, much would be required of them for the gift.

It has been said that, to whom much is given, much is required. God has given you much. Don't just think of money or tangible resources. Consider compassion, empathy, personal experiences, time, and love. God has given you more than you need of some things in your life. That is in order to enable you to give some of it away. The more you give, the more you'll have. You are specifically chosen for a certain job because of what God has given you. Romans 8:28 says, "We are assured and know that [God being a partner in their labor] all things work together and are [fitting into a plan] for good to and for those who love God and are called according to [His] design and purpose." From this we understand that everything you go through in your life, every experience, can be incorporated into the plan to produce something good. That means the good, the bad, and the ugly are all there to be used for good. We are all called according to his purpose. But, will we answer his call and allow everything that we

> God will cause all things to work together for your good. Your experiences are valuable.

have to be used for his purpose, the purpose of serving our fellow man?

What experiences have contributed to who you are today? What's in your house? What do you have to give? What abilities and gifts do you possess? Is it a friendly smile or a listening ear? Are you a great cook or good with children? Have you survived a common life challenge like divorce or death of a spouse? You have a lot to offer. Your life experiences, struggles, and successes all have equipped you with something to offer a person who is facing similar challenges. The best, and the worst, of your life experiences have prepared you to help another person. You would be surprised to know how appreciative people would be of your insight and the genuine empathy you can express because you've been through what they are going through. Just sharing your experience can provide comfort and encouragement to someone else. When you have already experienced a life challenge, you have a special understanding of the needs of someone who is going through that same challenge.

My mom had always been active in the church. As a child she attended Sunday school and sang in the choir. In her adult life, she made a deeper spiritual commitment and gave all of her spare time to church activities, volunteering, and holding office in various auxiliaries. After losing her husband to Leukemia and later retiring in her 60s, she found that she had a lot of time on her hands. All of her children were adults and she had no spouse to spend time with. The only person she was responsible for was my older sister, who was developmentally disabled, but very high-functioning. She did not have an active social life and was beginning to wonder what to do with herself sometimes.

At the time, I had been volunteeiing with an organization that did outreach to the homeless, aged, and indigent population in our area. I was finding great fulfillment in my volunteer work. So I had a talk with my mom.

I told my mom that she was wasting her time sitting around wondering what everyone else was doing. Many days when we talked on the phone, the conversation would go to which of my siblings didn't call her that day and who hadn't stopped by. After raising seven children, working, and volunteering at church for many years, she was not used to having so much time on her hands. Even though she worked out at the gym three days each week, attended a weekly Bible class, attended Sunday Worship Services, and visited with the family on the weekends, there was still a lot of down time to be accounted for. I told her that she had much to offer and that she should be so busy that we would have to make an appointment to see her.

I suggested that she would do well to donate some of her free time to the charity I was a part of. She had worked in healthcare services for many years and had spent a lot of time caring for the elderly. She planned many fundraising events and mentored several young women as a part of the church. She also raised a large family including a special needs child. I could go on. She was full of experience, skills, and wisdom that could be of great value to the community. She was on a fixed income and did not have money to give, but she had EVERYTHING else to offer. She decided to volunteer a couple of times each month and help out with events for special populations, and found great satisfaction in doing so. She met a really great group of people and also enjoyed setting up, serving food, and cleaning up after events. She enjoyed good company, good conversation, and good music while offering what she had to people who really needed her.

Sometimes we think we don't have much to give. But if you are alive, you have something to give. And believe me when I say that there are people in your community who would be honored and blessed if you would share your gifts with them.

## CHAPTER FOUR: YOU ARE THE SOLUTION

Luke 6:17-19

*17 And Jesus came down with them and took His stand on a level spot, with a great crowd of His disciples and a vast throng of people from all over Judea and Jerusalem and the seacoast of Tyre and Sidon, who came to listen to Him and to be cured of their diseases--*

*18 Even those who were disturbed and troubled with unclean spirits, and they were being healed [also].*

*19 And all the multitude were seeking to touch Him, for healing power was all the while going forth from Him and curing them all [saving them from severe illnesses or calamities].*

In this passage, Jesus came and presented himself to a huge mass of people. These people had come from all over to see him. They came to listen to him and they came because they knew that he had what they needed. They wanted to be near him and to touch him because he was the solution to their problems.  Emanating from him was the power and ability to cure everything that challenged them.  They were suffering from diseases, mental misery and spiritual distress.  And Jesus took the time to heal each one of them.

Problems are drawn toward their solutions and you are someone else's solution.  There will be no shortage of people who need what you have to offer. I promise you that if you stop, look and listen, you will find that opportunities to help others in your unique way are falling at your feet daily.  Sometimes we are so busy and caught up in the hustle of our ordinary day, whether it is a full-time job, running a business, or raising a family.  We are often so involved in our own lives that we don't take the time to even see those around us. But just know that the people who need you are close by.  You just have to pay attention if you truly want to see them. Listen to your heart. It will point them out to you.

Try to take just 5 or 10 minutes out of each day to stop, look, and listen.  It really doesn't matter where or when you do it.  Just follow your own intuition and do what feels right to you. Take a few minutes, *STOP* what you are doing, and be quiet. This will be the time that you take to *LOOK* for who in the world needs you. You may look around yourself and just visually survey your surroundings. See what catches your attention. Maybe something will draw your eye; an object, a bumper sticker, anything, or maybe nothing. You may be inspired to close your eyes and receive a visual impression from within. Let your imagination tell you how or where to *LOOK*.

Turn off the TV, or radio, and be in the silence or the natural sounds of your environment. If you are in the car, you might hear traffic sounds. If you are in the park, you might hear children playing. Whatever natural sounds are around you, it's okay. Just allow the sounds to blend in together. Then begin to *LISTEN* to the silence inside of you and not to your runaway thoughts about the rest of your day. Just *LISTEN* to the quiet inside of you. Because in that quiet place inside of you is the voice of your inspiration, the voice of your intuition, the voice of God. This voice is small and quiet. It will never interrupt your day and scream over all of the busy thoughts that crowd your mind. But if you take the time to stop everything and pay attention to it, it will have amazing things to tell you. It will inspire you toward great endeavors that will bless you and enrich your life.

You may receive a thought, feeling or idea right away, or you may not. It may come to you at another time. But you will have taken the time to *STOP* what you are doing, *LOOK* around and inside yourself, and

**Inside of you is the voice of inspiration. Be open to the inspiration when it comes.**

*LISTEN* to your heart. This simple action says that you are ready to see and hear what you need to know in order to help someone else. Just know that the person or people are within your reach, and you definitely have what they need. You may receive a phone call or an email that presents an opportunity to you. You may, at another time, come across an article in the newspaper or have a conversation with a stranger that leads to an idea. It doesn't matter how the inspiration comes to you, just be open to receive it when it comes.

Sometimes during my personal challenges, I felt I had nothing to give. With my marriage falling apart, I had so much sadness it would fill my days. Whether I was at my desk at work, driving the car, or sitting in church, the pain would become unbearable. Many times there was no way to stop the tears. But, I would have to press on for my children and for myself. The feelings of personal failure and public humiliation were overwhelming. I felt like there was nothing left for me. I was in survival mode. I had nothing to give. In the midst of all of this, other people's needs would keep presenting themselves to me. I would have to stop my own tears to focus on someone else's needs. Some of my close friends were hardworking, single mothers who also faced tough challenges. As a friend, I was able to encourage someone in a telephone call or help come up with last minute childcare ideas. Sometimes a friend might need encouragement through a personal crisis. When I was in a difficult marriage and a close friend was also in a difficult marriage, we both found a way to help each other through our personal storms. We provided advice, encouragement, and support for each other even though both of our lives were hard.

When I was divorced and lonely, I was able to encourage, advise, and pray for my married friends. Some of my greatest joys until this day are the strong, happy marriages of my dearest friends. I consider it a privilege to encourage and pray for them. I know what it feels like to go through a difficult marriage and divorce. I know how hard it is to be alone and raise children. I know the pain of losing my husband to an extramarital affair. Now that I have survived the whole ordeal, I have something unique to offer because of it. I never want to see someone else go through what I have been through. I don't want someone else's children to experience the loss that my children suffered. So I rejoice in the good marriages of my friends. I encourage them through difficult challenges. I pray for the continued health and happiness of their families. This is something that I have to give.

What you have to give may not always be a tangible thing like money. But, I can assure you that what you have to give is, nevertheless, valuable and sorely needed by someone who is within your reach at this moment. You have something important to give and someone will show up to receive it. If you stop, look, and listen to your heart, the need will become evident and you will possess the solution. In fact, you are the solution.

## CHAPTER FIVE: FOR THE LEAST OF THESE MY BROTHERS

Luke 6:20-23

*20 And solemnly lifting up His eyes on His disciples, He said: Blessed (happy--with life-joy and satisfaction in God's favor and salvation, apart from your outward condition--and to be envied) are you poor and lowly and afflicted (destitute of wealth, influence, position, and honor), for the kingdom of God is yours!*

*21  Blessed (happy--with life-joy and satisfaction in God's favor and salvation, apart from your outward condition--and to be envied) are you who hunger and seek with eager desire now, for you shall be filled and completely satisfied! Blessed (happy--with life-joy and satisfaction in God's favor and salvation, apart from your outward condition--and [k]to be envied) are you who weep and sob now, for you shall laugh!*

*22  Blessed (happy--with life-joy and satisfaction in God's favor and salvation, apart from your outward condition--and to be envied) are you when people despise (hate) you, and when they exclude and excommunicate you [as disreputable] and revile and denounce you and defame and cast out and spurn*

> *your name as evil (wicked) on account of the Son of Man.*
> 23 *Rejoice and be glad at such a time and exult and leap for joy, for behold, your reward is rich and great and strong and intense and abundant in heaven; for even so their forefathers treated the prophets.*

You are ultimately blessed by, in, and through your life experiences. I'm not pretending that it is easy to feel blessed when you are in the middle of the worst mess of your life. But in that mess resides your blessing and the blessings that you will share with others. In the above passage, Jesus made it clear to his disciples that it's okay to go through challenges in life. Challenges are a part of our human experience. However, within these challenges, blessings are woven throughout. He explained that even in the times when you cannot see it, God's favor is with you.

In the lifecycle of a plant, a seed dies away to produce a brand new plant. The new plant is the little seed multiplied into a new creation. Not only does it produce the new plant, but blossoms are produced for beauty, fruit for substance, and more precious seeds for reproduction. One little seed goes through this process to produce something beautiful and continual. Those new seeds will repeat the process and produce more plants and seeds and so on. Imagine a field of flowers. See the beauty. Then imagine all of the little seeds that died away to produce the beauty and the continuation of the meadow.

We are something like those seeds. When you become buried under one of life's challenges, you are like the little seed dying, with your outer shell falling away to make way for your new self. In this difficult process, you are becoming a new and better self. While, in the blessing of growing into your new self, you gain more to give and share with others for posterity. We come out of the experience like a new person with gifts to give to our fellow man and to pass on to future generations. The good that you derive from your experience will be passed on even after you are long gone.

Your experiences change you, but they change you for the better.

In Isaiah 61, verses 3 – 4, the Bible tells us what is in store for us when we go through the difficult times in our lives. Knowing that you have something wonderful to look forward to, gives you strength to meet your challenges with courage. Verse 3 says that God will grant us beauty for our ashes, joy for our mourning, and praise for our depression. The purpose of God granting us these good things is for us to be seen as great oak trees planted by God himself. Then verse 4 says we will rebuild the ruins, raise up former wastelands, and renew the ruined cities that have been that way for a long time. Just reading this promise from God makes an image in my mind of a forest that has been wiped out by fire. It becomes this devastated and desolate land; just black with ashes. But it's just a matter of time before you see new plant life start to appear out of the blackness. Little sprinkles of golden green foliage peek out of the charred earth. As the rain and the sunshine feed the land, time provides brand new, rich, beautiful land where there was nothing but ruins for a very long time. After the fire, the land probably looked like there was no life left there. But there is life. It's just under the ashes, and when the time comes, it will appear, more beautiful than ever.

Know that when you are going through something, you really are blessed. Your experiences change you, but they change you for the better. At the other end, you emerge a new and improved version of yourself with many gifts to share with others. Take what you have experienced and start a chain reaction of blessings that will continue into the future. What you have gone through will bless people who you may never even meet. Just know that you are blessed when you are destitute because you will soon live an abundant life and have more than you need. Then you can share your good fortune with others. You are blessed when you are hungry and searching for answers, because soon, you will have answers and you will be able to help someone else find the answers they search for. You are blessed when you are depressed and feeling hopeless, because you will be happy again. You are blessed when you feel left out and alone because of your situation.

You know the times when friends stop calling and coming by because they don't know what to say anymore. This scripture says that you should celebrate and be happy during these times. Find ways to enjoy yourself while you are still in the situation. Take some time to do something that you really like, a hobby or activity that you love. This will feed your spirit and help to ward off depression and loneliness. You want to try to be happy because you know that the very fact that you are meeting this challenge with courage means you are receiving wonderful gifts and blessings. They may not be visible yet. They may still be under the ashes; but nevertheless, they exist and they are yours for your trouble. But the single best part of all of this is that you will gain more tools with which to help others.

When you complete the challenge, when you emerge as your new and improved self, when your new self begins to grow, you have brand new tools in your life bag. You have experience, knowledge, compassion, and empathy that you didn't have before. You have solutions to problems. You have a road map of how to get through that situation that you can share with someone else. If you made it through unemployment and bankruptcy, you can help someone else who is in that situation. If you just made it through an unplanned pregnancy and birth with your teenage daughter, you are now able to help another devastated mother and daughter see the light at the end of their tunnel. These are all personal devastations, but if you weather them with perseverance, positivity, and determination, you can turn them into personal blessings that will ripple through future generations.

Have faith that your troubles are just paths to new beginnings. And if you can meet them with a positive outlook, there are millions of poor, hungry, sad, and socially outcast people who will be ultimately blessed by your actions. If you feel like you want to give up, maybe thinking of all the good you will do can be your encouragement. Matthew chapter 25, verses 35-40 explains that when we help someone in need, it's like we help Jesus himself, because we are all part of the same family. When you help your brother, you help yourself, and vise versa. Everything we do affects everyone else, so why not make a positive impact. Life comes in ebbs and flows. It's not always good and it's not always bad. Enjoy the good and meet the bad with a positive attitude and good determination. Have courage and you will become a positive influence on the world.

## CHAPTER SIX: IT'S NOT ABOUT YOU

Luke 6:24-26

*24  But woe to (alas for) you who are rich ([a]abounding*
*in material resources), for you already are receiving*
*your consolation (the solace and sense of*
*strengthening and cheer that come from prosperity)*
*and have taken and enjoyed your comfort in full*
*[having nothing left to be awarded you].*
*25  Woe to (alas for) you who are full now (completely*
*filled, luxuriously gorged and satiated), for you shall*
*hunger and suffer want! Woe to (alas for) you who*
*laugh now, for you shall mourn and weep and wail!*
*26  Woe to (alas for) you when everyone speaks fairly*
*and handsomely of you and praises you, for even so*
*their forefathers did to the false prophets.*

Now, as a personal practice, I usually try to accentuate the positive, but this subject needs to be covered.  So I will try to make it quick and painless.  In the last chapter, I talked about some of the horrible challenges any one of us might be faced with along our human journey. I also talked about how you should try to see that there are blessings hidden in those challenges. We just have to believe that, look for the blessings and when they begin to flow, SHARE THEM WITH OTHERS. You didn't think the blessings were for you, did you? Let me explain.

Again I want to talk about the concept of, "To whom much is given, much will be required". It comes from a passage in Luke chapter 12 where Jesus was teaching about a servant who can be trusted even when the master is away. He talks about the servant who is found awake and on task when the master returns and the servant who is found drunken and sleeping. So what does all of this have to do with anything that we have learned so far?

God appreciates when you use what He gives you to help others. That is why he gives you blessings. He prefers to see his children help one another by sharing with and caring for one another. So the good that you receive as a result of meeting your challenges with courage are not really for you. They are entrusted to you for the benefit of others. So it's really a question of whether or not you can be trusted with these blessings. Let's think back to the little seed that has to die away to produce a beautiful flower or a mighty oak.

So you go through the worst difficulty of your life and you emerge as that beautiful flower, or that mighty oak. That's really great for you. But what happens if you just stand there soaking up sun and rain, just growing and blooming and loving your new life. What happens if you, the flower, never drop your seeds and never allow a bee to use your pollen to pass along? You will never bring about that beautiful meadow. You will be one flower that dies away and is forgotten. The same with becoming that mighty oak, if you never drop your acorns and allow them to germinate along side of you, you will not be the instigator of a great forest. You will only be a beautiful oak for a while and then you die. But what if you enjoy your new self, but make it your mission to seek out people who need what you have and share it with them? Then you are guaranteed to eventually become a beautiful meadow, or a great forest, to the glory of God. Your seeds can be passed on and on into the future and contribute to something wonderfully beyond what you can even imagine. Ephesians chapter 19 verse 20 tells us that God "is able to do superabundantly, far over and above all that we ask or think". So by following his plan of using what you have to serve others, you are setting your life up for an experience that promises to be more remarkable than anything that you can dream.

Remember: To whom much is given, much will be required.

So in the above passage, we are told that when we take our good fortune and use it only to increase ourselves, to make our lives more luxurious and comfortable, that is our total reward. There is no need to look for anything more because you have made your purpose to serve yourself and not others. There is no further reward for you.

When we make it through our challenges, it might be easy to sit back and be comfortable when the blessing follow. But if we just wallow in our personal contentment and rejoice in our new happy state without considering why we have been blessed with new happiness and contentment, we put ourselves in danger of returning to the same pain and struggle. The way to perpetuate your good fortune is to share it with others.

I cannot tell you how mind-boggling it can be when you are in a terrible life struggle that is threatening to overwhelm you and some unexpected person appears with relief. Your first reaction is a little bit of confusion as you ask yourself what just happened. As you comprehend that someone has come to your rescue, you want to know why. Then, because you trust in God's infinite wisdom to guide your life, you realize that it was just one of those ordinary miracles that happen and go unnoticed each day. Finally, you feel the gratitude and wonder as you realize God's providence in your own life. Take note of how you felt when providence touched you. You will soon have your chance to play the opposite role for someone else. It is a wonderful thing to receive, but even more fulfilling to give. Look forward for your turn to play the role of the giver.

Final word of advice on this subject... don't look for any recognition at all when you share your good fortune with others. I know it's sometimes impossible to stop people from thanking you and patting you on the back, but don't look for it. And when it happens, receive it quietly and with humility. Many times you might not even receive a thank you. Don't take it personal. Try to remember how low you felt when you were going through your problems. Think back to how hopeless you felt sometimes. This will put it all into perspective. It's not always easy to say thank you. Sometimes receiving an unselfish act of kindness can be so unexpected and overwhelming, that you can't say anything. Many times people have thoughts like, "How will I ever repay you?" And that even causes anxiety. When you do an act of kindness, try to gently convey that you are not looking for thanks or repayment. Your joy is in the fact that you were able to help.

Ultimately, being well spoken of really means nothing. Many people are well spoken of and lack both character and good will. People are given prestige for all kinds of accomplishments, both good and bad. How many times have you seen the face of a convicted murderer being glorified on a T-shirt? Having the recognition of people means nothing. The real rewards are the good that you do, and knowing that you make a difference.

So keep in mind that you are blessed in order to bless others who are in need. It is given to you so that you may give. You will enjoy your life's good fortune, but you will enjoy it more completely when you share it with others.

## CHAPTER SEVEN:  WHO NEEDS YOU

<u>Luke 6:27-31</u>

27  *But I say to you who are listening now to Me: [in
order to heed, make it a practice to] love your
enemies, treat well (do good to, act nobly toward)
those who detest you and pursue you with hatred,*

28  *Invoke blessings upon and pray for the happiness of
those who curse you, implore God's blessing (favor)
upon those who abuse you [who revile, reproach,
disparage, and high-handedly misuse you].*

29  *To the one who strikes you on the jaw or cheek,
offer the other jaw or cheek also; and from him who
takes away your outer garment, do not withhold your
undergarment as well.*

30  *Give away to everyone who begs of you [who is in
want of necessities], and of him who takes away
from you your goods, do not demand or require them
back again.*

31  *And as you would like and desire that men would
do to you, do exactly so to them.*

When Jesus was here on Earth living His human experience, He reached out to everyone. He did not pick and choose only those people who would be easy to deal with. But, he did reach out to those who needed him, those who needed what he had to give. He did not take into consideration their social status or how it would reflect on him to be associated with them.

In the Bible (Luke 19:1-10), we find the story of a man named Zacchaeus who was a tax collector. In fact, he was described as chief tax collector. In this time, tax collectors were notorious for abusing their position and taking advantage of the citizens in order to become wealthy. They were generally hated and treated as outcasts among the Jews because they were dishonest and worked for the Roman government. So Zacchaeus, although a rich man, was a social outcast. He is described as a short man and undoubtedly lived a lonely existence.

When Zacchaeus heard that Jesus was coming his way he climbed a sycamore tree in order to be able to see above the crowd. He just wanted to get a glimpse of Jesus. When Jesus passed his way, he looked up and saw Zacchaeus in the tree. He called to Zacchaeus by name and told him to hurry down because he would be visiting his house that day. The crowd of onlookers was appalled by this. How could Jesus even talk to such a person, much less spend time in his home? But Jesus was not concerned with any of that. He knew he had something that Zacchaeus needed that day.

The story goes on to tell us that because Jesus decided to visit with him that day, Zacchaeus vowed to give half of his possessions to the poor and to pay back anyone he had cheated four times what he owed them to make it right. Not only was Zacchaeus' life completely changed by Jesus' actions, but we don't know how far the effects rippled beyond that day. I believe an act of kindness can ripple on indefinitely like when you drop a pebble in a pool of still water and it begins many waves that ripple out across the water in every direction. The story only tells us that Jesus visited with Zacchaeus in his house, that's all. It doesn't tell us anything else that he did for Zacchaeus that day. But that one visit caused Zacchaeus to make a significant contribution to needy people in the community as well as repay (at considerable interest) money he had stolen from citizens. What a tremendous blessing that must have been throughout the community! And we have no idea how far that blessing continued to other people, other families, and even other communities. Jesus going against the status quo and doing what he needed to do initiated a chain of blessings for everyone, even for the people who hated Zacchaeus.

There are many such stories in the New Testement where Jesus ministered to people who were shunned by society. He did not let class, gender, or race deter him from reaching those who needed his help. It was not only poor people, but also rich – not only men, but women too – not only Jews, but Samaritans – priests and Pharisees as well as the multitudes, none of that mattered. Jesus took time with everyone because they needed his help. He cared for people regardless of their station in life. He understood them.

Jesus understood that people develop certain attitudes, behaviors, and coping mechanisms as a result of their life experiences. We all develop our behaviors and outlook based on our own unique experiences in life. Children of single parents often have a different approach to life than those that were raised in two parent households. People who have grown up in a financially secure situation see life differently than those who have experienced poverty. And each of us have our own reactions and draw our own conclusions from what we have experienced in the past as well as our present circumstances. I don't believe we should judge our brothers and sisters for the way they react to life's many challenges, especially if you have not shared that same challenge. You never know how you would respond to the situation. So all we can do is take people for who they are and where they are at this moment. We should give others the benefit of the doubt that they are coping as best they can in the given situation.

Imagine, if you can, being a homeless mother with small children. As you struggle through each day with your children, how might you feel as a mother, as a person? Your children look to you for every comfort; food, shelter, love, and security. It is your responsibility, not only to care for them, but to introduce them to the world around them and prepare them for life. And here you are, unable to provide the very basic necessities. How might you feel and what thoughts go through your head as you go through your day, sitting in the park all day wondering how you will provide a meal today or where you will sleep tonight; knowing that your children are cold or hungry and you can't figure out a way to meet their needs? I'm sure in the course of the day you see other families in passing – families of parents and well dressed children who ride in minivans with DVD players. It may appear to you that other people enjoy every comfort of life and take it all for granted. You might see others pass you on the street and either ignore you and your family or even worse, give that look of pity and disgust before they look away. So how to do feel and what do you think all day?

People
need
hope,
love
&
compassion.

Imagine the animosity you might feel toward others. Maybe you hate the man whose absence has made this situation possible. Maybe you resent the general public for having more than you and not caring enough to help you. Maybe you resent the social and community workers that you have to go to everyday for help – for a meal or a pair of shoes or diapers – because the fact that you have to go to them makes you feel like a loser. Do you begin to resent your children because they are a constant reminder of your failure? Imagine the hopelessness you might feel for yourself, your children, and the future. How you got into this situation becomes somewhat irrelevant in the scheme of your daily life. How might this shape your relationship to and perception of people and life in general? Will you begin to hate and despise others because you feel hated and despised by them? Will you become calloused and lack compassion because you do not experience compassion in your own life? What kind of person does this make you? You are depressed and angry, but ultimately you are a victim of circumstance who is in need of hope, love, and compassion.

I love to watch documentaries on all sorts of issues and topics. I recently watched a documentary that chronicled a hardworking, divorced, single mom who had 4 or 5 school-aged children. Their family lived in a tough, urban neighborhood. The mom did everything on her own, working outside the home in addition to actively parenting her children. From the very beginning of this documentary, I was rooting for this mom. She would rise early in the morning rallying the troupes to baths, breakfast and book bags. She would get everyone off to school with all their needs met before she headed off to her job for the day. At her job, she was pleasant, hardworking, and respected by her coworkers. In every respect, this mother was a great person, a committed parent with economically challenging circumstances. So when a friend referred her to a community housing program that could help her become a homeowner, I was happy to see her get a much deserved hand up to a better life.

This community program was a godsend. It provided every service needed to help a family move to a better neighborhood, better housing, and a better economic situation. A volunteer within the program would walk through every step with the client to clear up minor credit issues, secure a down payment, and qualify for a mortgage. The program was a resource that supported the client right up to move in day. The house would be a new construction in a newly developed part of the city. The community would be comprised of all new homeowners and their families. The homes were beautiful. Watching this story unfold, I thought this couldn't happen to a better person. I thought this mom was well deserving of such help because she was a great mom with great children who would go far in life with a little help. I could see that participation in this program could be a stepping stone to a better life for this and future generations of this nice family. Wow, if this could just happen for more people!

As the documentary went on, I watched this mom, as she continued her daily life of work and family responsibilities. Like every good mom she handled homework, groceries, meals, family-time, housecleaning, etc. In addition, she had regular meetings and phone calls with her mentor at the community program. Under the mentor's guidance, I watched her take care of various financial tasks, paying off debts, acquiring financial documents, and providing everything that was asked of her to meet program deadlines. I was like a cheerleader rooting for her at every turn, as she worked her way through the process.

Then, something unexpected happened. The process became overwhelming for this great mom. She started to become nervous about the whole thing. I thought this was understandable. When you embark upon something in life that you have never done before, like buying your first home, it can make you nervous. I think it's just human nature to be a little apprehensive in new situations. Usually, we have to summon courage and push ourselves through these times.

The closer this mother came to the realization of the dream of homeownership, the more she became gripped by fear and disbelief. She had trouble wrapping her brain around the reality of it all. Soon she became frozen in the process and unable to move forward. She started missing appointments and failing to return calls from her mentor. I found this puzzling because she had done well so far and this was the eleventh hour. I couldn't understand why she would blow this opportunity. I continued to watch the story unfold.

I felt frustration watching the mother back away from a great opportunity for her family. I wanted to yell at her and shake some sense into her. "Are you kidding me? What are you thinking?" I just couldn't believe that she could let this slip through her fingers. She was much too smart to do that. I kept watching and my frustration turned to disbelief as the mentor called in a good friend of the mother. This was the friend who recommended the mother for the program.

The friend took the mother to the newly-constructed home and went inside. She showed her the reality of what she might be passing on. She pleaded with her to face her fears and stay the course. But this poor mother had become terrified of the unfamiliar and unknown. Although she had trouble articulating her specific concerns about the whole plan, she did express a kind of confusion. This was all too good to be true. And, in her experience, that meant it could not be true.

My heart was breaking when I began to realize that the fear that gripped her was based in disbelief. The truth is that she had no prior life experience to which she could associate this situation. No one had ever reached out to her in such a profound way, and why would they? In her life, she had worked hard for everything and disappointment was par for the course. The truth is that she was much more emotionally prepared for the whole deal to fall through than she was prepared for it to succeed. She knew how to handle loss and disappointment. She hadn't a lot of experience with success.

It just didn't make any sense to her that ANYONE would do so much to help her family in such a big way. What were they getting out of helping her? She could not envision her life changing so dramatically. What you cannot imagine, simply cannot happen. The community worker provided help, mentorship, compassion, dignity, and genuine friendship. But with all of that support, this hard-working, loving mother backed out of the program at the eleventh hour and the house went to another family.

As I sat watching the conclusion of the documentary, I wasn't sure how to feel. It was a sad ending for the mother and children who I had been hoping to see move to a better life and a brighter future. I wanted to see a happy ending, but in life, many endings are not happy. It was a lesson to me. The documentary gave me a small glimpse into a world that was beyond my personal experience. I felt compassion for the mother and her children. I wished there had been some way that she could have accepted what was probably the greatest blessing of her life.

I used to think that being a mother gave me an understanding of mothers, but that is not necessarily true. In some ways, my motherhood experience helps me to understand mothers. In other cases though, my own motherhood experience is not much help at all.

I remember when I was an elementary school teacher for a short time some years ago. I had a classroom of twenty young children from an "at risk" population. This was a community with many social challenges that were beyond my personal experience. Among my precious young students were many family situations. Parental involvement in school was all but nonexistent, but there were two mothers who will always stand out in my memory because they taught me something.

The mothers of two little girls in my class had problems with drug addiction. I am positive that more parents of other students also suffered from this plague of the community, but these two moms were special. During the months that I had the privilege of teaching their daughters, they both stood out as involved and attentive parents.

Both of these mothers were nice ladies and I liked them on a personal level. They were concerned parents and made their best effort to take good care of their children. Both of their daughters had good attendance, were well-groomed, and received good nutrition. These women tried hard to be good mothers and were the most (if not the only) involved parents of my class. Nevertheless, drug addiction was a ruling factor and ongoing struggle in their lives.

As I interacted with them occasionally, and with their precious little daughters daily, they taught me a lot. Although we had motherhood in common, the struggle of drug addiction was beyond my realm of experience. In my naiveté, I had thought that addicts were selfish and uncaring. I thought they all lived for drugs and neglected and/or abused their children. I'm sure I had some resentment for "these people" I knew nothing about because I thought "they" should make better choices for themselves and their children. However, knowing the two moms changed my perspective greatly.

Knowing and observing them and their children gave me a window into a world that was not a part of my personal experience. I learned how much they truly loved their children by the sincere efforts they made to be good mothers. I got to know them and I liked them. I loved their beautiful daughters and I felt compassion for them in their struggles with drug addiction.

After knowing these moms and their children, I could no longer pass judgment on people because of drug addiction. I realized that those preconceptions I had held were based in ignorance to a world I knew nothing about. I taught their children, but they also became my teachers in a more profound way and I am grateful for the lessons they taught me.

I learned that it is not good to assume to understand someone's heart, especially when their experience is different than yours. I understood that I should accept people for who they are and where they are in life because we are all, ultimately, the same. Our challenges may be different, but at the core, we are human. That's all that matters.

The hierarchy of who's better than whom, of the haves and the have nots, is all man-made. All people need acceptance and to be valued as human no matter what their circumstances may be. We must see people as our brothers and sisters and give them the same respect that we would expect to receive.

## CHAPTER EIGHT: PAYING FORWARD

### Luke 6:32-36

*32 If you [merely] love those who love you, what quality of credit and thanks is that to you? For even the [very] sinners love their lovers (those who love them).*

*33 And if you are kind and good and do favors to and benefit those who are kind and good and do favors to and benefit you, what quality of credit and thanks is that to you? For even the preeminently sinful do the same.*

*34 And if you lend money at interest to those from whom you hope to receive, what quality of credit and thanks is that to you? Even notorious sinners lend money at interest to sinners, so as to recover as much again.*

*35 But love your enemies and be kind and do good [doing favors so that someone derives benefit from them] and lend, expecting and hoping for nothing in return but considering nothing as lost and despairing of no one; and then your recompense (your reward) will be great (rich, strong, intense, and abundant), and you will be sons of the Most High, for He is kind and charitable and good to the ungrateful and the selfish and wicked.*

*36 So be merciful (sympathetic, tender, responsive, and compassionate) even as your Father is [all these].*

The greatest lesson the moms in the previous chapter taught me is that we cannot use someone's life situation to pass judgment on them. The mother in the documentary taught me that we have to consider a person's past experiences and personal outlook when we want to help them. Some people are difficult to help and some problems are complex beyond our understanding. Some people are reluctant to accept your help and you don't know why. Some people might resent you. Others may be emotionally unprepared for what you are offering. If you wish to help someone in a real way, you will need humility and most of all patience.

Realize that you don't know everything and that <u>any person</u> can have something to teach you, if you pay attention; observe, listen, and be patient. Even though you are the one who is in the position to help someone, you must be careful to treat people the way you want to be treated. You have to be sure to preserve a person's dignity. Sometimes you'll find an opportunity to even restore someone's dignity.

Let me explain. There are ways to help and meet a primary need. But if we slow down and think, we might be able to meet more needs in the same act of kindness. For example, a parent might be grateful if you buy school clothes for his or her children. But that same parent and children can feel good about doing their own school shopping with a gift card that you discreetly provided. Your discretion and the opportunity for the family to do something the same as other families, preserves the dignity of that family. Such a small adjustment may even restore some of the lost self-esteem of that parent and children.

No one wants to feel like someone else's charity case. Sometimes receiving can make a person feel worse, not better. Even in being grateful for the help, a person can feel more helpless and depressed at the fact that they are unable to help his or her self. We have to be careful to remember that the purpose of giving is not to make you feel good about yourself (that's just a nice side-effect). The purpose is to enhance the life of another by doing something that they are unable to do for themselves. In doing this, you must endeavor to give dignity, self-worth, hope, and success along with your tangible gifts. Make sure the receiving is as wonderful an experience as the giving.

Be careful not to take anything away in the process of your giving. It defeats the purpose of your charity. When I lost my corporate job in 2002, it kicked off a whole chain of challenges for my children and me. I lost my income, savings, and retirement. Over the months following, my car broke down and was repossessed by the bank. I had to sell my house to avoid foreclosure. I had to enroll my children in public school for the first time because I could no longer pay tuition for private school. I lost our medical, dental and life insurance. I lost and lost and lost – month by month -- I lost. I am a strong person, but continuous loss over a long period of time makes anyone feel like a loser. To go from a hard-working parent to a total loser is depressing, demoralizing, and degrading.

While I had no insurance, the schools were demanding medical check-ups for my two daughters. So the school nurse referred me to a local free clinic. It was difficult to get in touch with them or to get an appointment. I eventually made it to the initial screening where I had to go in, answer questions, and fill out a lot of forms. A nice gentleman was sitting in an office with me conducting the process. He and I were completing forms together when he was called away and another volunteer came in to take over. I don't remember if she said, "Hello" to me or if she introduced herself. She sat down at the desk and went straight to the forms. She organized them and proceeded to hand me some forms to fill out when she stopped to ask, "You know how to read and write, don't you?"

I was so stunned I was speechless. Her words seemed to hit me in the center of my chest and I never saw it coming. For a few seconds, I couldn't form a response. I just sat with a shocked expression and my mouth open. Finally, I was able to say, "Yes." But, what I wanted to say was, "How dare you!" I was insulted, hurt, appalled, and sorry for the other people that would come in contact with this person. As I later recounted the experience to friends, I wondered who could listen to one sentence from my mouth and not be sure that I was literate. But then I realized that no one had been listening that day.

At our subsequent appointment at the clinic with the volunteer pediatrician, I found the young, female doctor to be somewhat condescending. She was polite and attentive but spoke to me in a way that someone might address a child or a person of low intellect. She discussed my daughter's approaching puberty as if I knew nothing about the subject and did very little listening. It felt more like a lecture than an examination. I realize and admit that I was hypersensitive to the whole situation of someone thinking less of me because of my financial status. Nevertheless, I was both grateful for the service and insulted by the treatment I received.

Give dignity, hope, self-worth, success.

The people who worked in that clinic were doing a noble service, providing medical care for people in need. The economic climate in the community was worsening and many working families were uninsured. Referred to as the "working poor" the community really benefitted from this outreach. All of the doctors and support staff volunteered their services to help the community. However, I believe some of them had preconceived notions of who the patients were and passed judgment on them without even knowing them. I don't think they counted on meeting me or people like me. So when I walked in the door, someone had already decided who and what I was. How sad.

If we are going to reach out and offer help to people who need us, we must realize that passing judgment on them is not only wrong, it is counterproductive. Passing judgment only creates and feeds resentment. In many cases, people in need grow accustomed to being treated without respect and dignity. They understand that in the eyes of some people, they are of low worth and are the invisible members of the community. They can feel it when people look down on them with pity and disgust. If you fell on hard times because of factors beyond your control, would you not resent having to assume this low position in society? I did.

I feel like I am belaboring the point, but please bear with me while I conclude with a strong admonition. If you will begin your human purpose of reaching out to your fellow man, I believe these are the most important things to remember. It goes beyond any tangible gift you may have to offer. First, prepare yourself emotionally and mentally. Go deep inside to find all of your compassion and understanding. Prepare your mind for the experience and then follow the example that Jesus set for us.

Endeavor to love people. Be kind, do good, and leave the rest up to God. Be merciful the way God has been merciful to you. Trust that He will enable you to do everything He has called you to do. This is paying it forward; giving of yourself without expectations.

*Let us not be satisfied with just giving money. Money is not enough, money can be got, but they need your hearts to love them. So, spread your love everywhere you go.*
*~Mother Teresa*

## CHAPTER NINE:  GIVING BACK

Luke 6:37-38

*37 Judge not [neither pronouncing judgment nor
subjecting to censure], and you will not be judged; do
not condemn and pronounce guilty, and you will not
be condemned and pronounced guilty; acquit and
forgive and [a]release (give up resentment, let it drop),
and you will be acquitted and forgiven and
[b]released.
38 Give, and [gifts] will be given to you; good measure,
pressed down, shaken together, and running over,
will they pour [c]into [the pouch formed by] the bosom
[of your robe and used as a bag]. For with the
measure you deal out [with the measure you use
when you confer benefits on others], it will be
measured back to you.*

In the previous chapters, I talked about putting
yourself aside in order to effectively offer yourself (your
gifts) to someone who really needs you.  I talked about
having empathy for the other person, trying to identify

with what they must be going through and also realizing that there are some things that we just cannot understand. But, when you are forgiving and non-judgmental in your approach, you open yourself up to amazing possibilities for profound experiences. Through these experiences, you will achieve real personal growth.

In reaching out to help someone, we should have no judgment of them, their situation, or how they came to be in need. All of those things are irrelevant. If a person arrives by ambulance to the emergency room bleeding, the doctors and nurses first assess the injury and then proceed directly to the course of treatment that will stabilize the person's condition. They don't have a consultation to find out how and why the person became injured. They don't discuss whether or not the person deserves medical attention. The original Hippocratic Oath states, "I will prescribe regimens for the good of my patients according to my ability and my judgment and never do harm to anyone." No part of the oath says a doctor should judge whether or not a patient deserves medical attention. And this has to be our attitude toward others. If you encounter someone who is in need, you should only assess what the need is and then decide upon a course of action that will meet the need. We are not judges. If you feel negatively toward the person or their plight, you should excuse yourself from the situation altogether. It is obviously not the case for you to handle. Your negative judgment will impede you from freely sharing your gifts.

So this is what verse 37 tells us, do not judge one another. It goes on to say that if we do not judge others, then we will not be judged by others. If we do not criticize others, then we will not be criticized by others. If we are forgiving to others, we will be forgiven by others. What a lovely spiritual principal. You get what you give. It's the old golden rule that we all learned in the Primary class in Sunday School:

*"So then, whatever you desire that others would do to and for you, even so do also to and for them..." ~Matthew 7:12*

Do unto others as you would have them do unto you.

This is also the principal of sowing and reaping. The seeds you plant will determine what will grow in your life. If you plant apples, then apples will grow. If you plant dandelions, dandelions will grow. When you give forgiveness and understanding, then you will receive forgiveness and understanding.  When you judge and criticize, you will ultimately be judged and criticized. What you give is what you will receive. That's the bottom line.

In 2001, I was divorced and raising three wonderful children.  By that point, my life had taken all kinds of twists and turns that I had not anticipated.  I had recently landed a good job, by the grace of God and was making ends meet.  My oldest and middle children were both attending a small, Christian school where I was a very involved parent-volunteer.  Even though I worked full-time, I dedicated every free minute to helping out at their school. That summer, the children were attending the school's summer camp that provided extraordinary experiences for the students.  One of the scheduled activities was a visit to a recording studio hosted by Bruce Springsteen.  The children would rehearse a couple of songs and record them at the studio as a part of their learning experience.  Since singing is a passion of mine, I had been asked to do a lead vocal on one of the songs with the children.  Of course I said yes.  I was the mom who participated in everything.

I was used to squeezing out time from work to spend with the children at camp or school. So, on the day of the recording, I went to my office for the morning.   Then, I left and met the children at the recording studio that afternoon.  It was a fun day for the kids.  We met the studio owner, musicians, staff, and Mr. Springsteen.  We went into the sound booth and recorded the background vocals of the songs.  Then everyone left the sound booth and I stayed to record my lead vocals.  It was a lot of fun.  It had been years since I had been in a recording studio.  Since I had been married and started a family, I hadn't found much time for music.  So being back in the studio was a little intimidating, but very exciting for me.  I was well rehearsed and all warmed up.  I really liked the song too.  I sang one take on the lead vocal track and it was done.  Wow, so much fun!  I took off the headset and came out of the sound booth.  The studio staff congratulated    me    on    my    performance.     Mr. Springsteen gave me a big hug and told me I did a great job.   It felt good to add my voice to the children's project that day. Music was something that I had to give. It didn't cost me anything but time.

As a result of me lending my help to the camp's musical project that day, I met Bruce Springsteen and also met a man named Tim McLoone. Tim was the founder of a local charitable organization in New Jersey called Holiday Express.

Holiday Express consists of a group of local musicians and volunteers who spend their time during the holiday season each year delivering the gift of human kindness to people who are in need. Through music, food, and gifts, these people show love in a very real way to others who are homeless, in shelters, hospitals, nursing facilities and in otherwise grim circumstances.

The day I met Mr. McLoone at the recording studio, he invited me to join the Holiday Express organization as a singer with the band. That was the beginning of something wonderful in my life.

The previous five years of my life had been filled with turmoil. There had been fighting, divorce, and depression. I and my children had been through the ringer and back again. In the summer of 2001, my children were 3, 7, and 11 years old. My focus was to do everything I could to improve their quality of life. They were in private school. They went to summer camp. They played sports, took dance classes, and went on family vacations. No matter how difficult life had become for me, I put everything I had into giving them a great life. That was my goal and responsibility. So by going to the studio to sing that afternoon, I was sowing what I had into my children. When Mr. McLoone asked me to join his organization, my seeds had begun to grow.

A couple of months later, I joined Holiday Express and met many wonderful people. I made new friends and gained an outlet to sing again. I could sing as often as I wanted and I could bring my children along. As a part of the band, I had 50+ opportunities each year to get in front of an audience and sing, sing, sing! I gave music to people who needed my help and I received more music and more ways to give more music... more, more, more! As if that wasn't a big enough blessing, God allowed me to meet two people who would have had a great impact on my life through their love, friendship, and *MUSIC*.

The first two band members I met were a mother and daughter, Delores and Layonne Holmes. I will never meet two more wonderful friends in life. Right from the beginning, the three of us felt like family. We had an instant connection, musically and otherwise. Delores and Layonne took me under their wings and welcomed me to the group. Soon, I was going out to see them perform with Mr. McLoone's band, "Tim McLoone and the Shirleys". Before this, I really didn't have a social life anymore. I just spent all of my time being a mom.

Delores and I became fast friends. We talked on the phone and emailed each other a lot. Within a few months, the ladies invited me to take a weekend trip with them and a group of musicians. My mother encouraged me to go because I rarely took time for myself, away from my children. The getaway was more fun than I could have imagined. The three of us had great fun together exploring, singing, and laughing a lot. That weekend, we all realized that we shared a special bond.

We later went on a Caribbean cruise together to celebrate my 40th birthday and in the fall of 2002, we started our own band called RAIN. For the next eight years the three of us sang together as RAIN. Being a part of RAIN was life-changing for me. We hung out, rehearsed, performed and traveled together. I felt like the adopted sister of the Holmes ladies. We had a harmonic sound that Delores often described as organic. People always asked us if I was related to them because of that special sound. It was just kismet. Holiday Express and RAIN were gifts that brought endless music into my life. It was more than I could have ever expected to receive. I gave music without any expectations, but because of my giving, I met celebrities, sang in major concert venues, made television and radio appearances, earned a supplemental income, and was blessed in too many ways to remember. I didn't receive only music, I also received friendship and kindness.

During this same period of time, the world was changing and I would enter another major life challenge. When six months after the September 11th terrorist attacks on the World Trade Center, I lost my job, I had very little savings and no other means of support. Losing my job took the wind out of my sails. I had already been through so much, I just didn't know if I could survive another major setback. Although I tried to summon my courage, regroup and persevere, it was a major blow to my existence. Once again, the rug had been pulled out from under me and I was trying to keep my chin up and work through the devastation.

I collected unemployment, went to graduate school, and tried diligently to provide for my family. But, it was difficult and depressing. After unemployment and savings had all dried up, I was left with no means of income. Child support payments from my ex-husband had also stopped. The economy was getting worse and there were no jobs to be found. With two degrees, 20 years of work experience, and a teaching certificate, I could not find adequate employment. My house was heading into foreclosure and I was struggling to keep food on the table.

This may have been the darkest time of my life. I slipped into a depression. It was difficult to get up in the morning, difficult to take a shower, difficult to take care of my children. The simplest tasks had become very hard to do. I had to enroll my children in public school for the first time. At every turn there was a new challenge. Money, cars, food, bills, and mortgage payments were all daily challenges. I regularly had different services and utilities shut off for non-payment. In the summer, the gas company would shut off my service. So there was no gas for hot water or cooking. I went to the local food bank for food. We had become one of those families on the charity lists to receive gifts and food at the holidays. For the first time ever, I experienced a Christmas when I could not buy any gifts for my children. That was hard.

Most people around me had no idea about the depth of my situation. For me, it was all very embarrassing. I didn't want everyone to know the mess I was in. Only my closest friends really knew the desperation of my circumstances. Through all of this, I tried to make it on my own, but it was impossible. So there were people who came forward and helped us. These people were not the people you would expect to become my rescuers. They were actually those who you would least expect.

The bank was beginning foreclosure on my home and I had no means with which to avoid the action. I had another friend in similar circumstances who had sold her home to avoid foreclosure. So I was seeking a way to do the same thing. I was referred to someone who was a member with me on the board of the private school that my children had attended. I hoped he would be able to help me sell my house. I had no idea where we would go, but at the very least, maybe I could avoid foreclosure.

By this time, I had been living in my home for 10 years. During that time, I had regularly opened my home to close friends and family members who had fallen upon hard times and needed a place to stay. On at least 7 different occasions in those 10 years, I had taken people in to live with us. Some were single moms with young children. Some were just a friend or family member. Some stayed a few months. Some had stayed a few of years. I had also been in the habit of regularly taking in children from the school whose mothers needed a place for them to stay for a few days or a week or two. My house was kind of a safe haven and I liked it that way. In all, these women and children temporarily became a part of our family and we enjoyed the company. It was a chance for me to help and encourage those who I cared about at tough times in their lives. It was also nice having another adult in the house to talk to sometimes.

So with my bank now proceeding with foreclosure, I thought long and hard about what to do. I tried to weigh my options, but I didn't have any. I tried to think of anything else that I could do. I, being super-resourceful, had always been able to come up with a plan. But this time, I was at a complete loss. I couldn't believe that I was in this position for the third time in 10 years, facing the possibility of having no house for my children and didn't know where we would go.

My home had been in jeopardy two times before, once with the county sheriff at my door serving me papers. In those instances, God had been gracious and guided me out of the situation. Each time, I made a deal with the bank and was able to save my home. There had never been anyone there to help me but God. Now, I found that there was nothing I could do.

I couldn't find a way out, no open doors. God had a different plan.

I stood in my kitchen one day contemplating my dilemma and fighting tears. My children were at school. I finally summoned my courage, swallowed hard and made the phone call that I had been dreading for weeks. I called the man I knew from the school board. I told him that I wanted his help to sell my home because my mortgage was behind and the bank was foreclosing. It was hard to hear myself say the words. It felt like surrendering to defeat. I remember the lump in my throat, the sick feeling in the pit of my stomach and wanting to cry. No tears though. I feared that if I ever allowed tears to fall, I would fall apart completely and there would be nothing left of me. I will never forget that phone call and how difficult it was for me to make it. But that difficult phone call turned out to be the door that God was opening for me, the same way I had opened my door to others who needed help. The person I called that day, who barely knew me, became a friend and an unexpected resource in my life.

Immediately, he told me that it would not be necessary to sell my home and there were other options to be exhausted before that decision had to be made. What?! Was this some kind of a miracle? Within the week, my mortgage was current and I was working with a referral who was guiding me through a tangle of social services that could help me keep my house. Eventually, I received services that I had not known existed. They paid my mortgage current, provided food, medical coverage and a cash stipend for six months. Let me not sugar-coat this process. It was welfare and it was not fun.

You are the gift.

I found the process to be humiliating, degrading, and uncomfortable. I encountered many raised eyebrows and questions like, "You live *WHERE?*" and "...finishing a *MASTERS DEGREE?*" I was a perfectly healthy, intelligent and educated woman with many talents. The public welfare system didn't expect to see clients like me, and I never expected to find myself there either. Unemployment had been hard enough, but welfare?

How did I get here?  What did I do wrong?  Hadn't I worked hard enough?  Wasn't I a responsible person? Didn't I always do my best to take care of myself, family, and others?  Why was this happening to me?

There were many days that I found myself wallowing in self-pity, but I would soon be reminded that I had much to be thankful for.  I didn't have a job and my children didn't have private school anymore. But what I had was more time with my children, a stable home, and a means to take care of us for a while.  I had to make a choice to focus on what I had or on what was missing.  Each day, I had to make the decision to see the glass half full or half empty, to notice the clouds or the rays of sun peeking through. Some days were better than others.  But through prayer, friendship, and perseverance, I made the best of it.  My children were my responsibility and a source of strength for me.  It was my goal and focus to make their childhood a fun and happy one.  I tried in every way possible to shield them from the problems we all faced.  Together, we made it from day to day, week to week, month to month, and time passed.

I ultimately forged a professional relationship and lasting friendship with the person who had helped to save my house from foreclosure. Although I was out of work for many years (yes, YEARS), I was able to consult for his businesses and collaborate on strategies to help my situation. I performed regularly with RAIN and spent holiday seasons volunteering with Holiday Express. It was not a lucrative existence, but it was survival, and I was thankful for the resources in my life.

I still live in the same house today. I have not since had to deal with the threat of foreclosure. I am not saying it was easy, but I am a witness to the faithfulness of God and His spiritual laws. I have often given a roof, a meal, gifts, etc. to those in need. So I never had to be without a roof, a meal or my children without Christmas gifts thanks to the spiritual law of giving. God is faithful to His word.

This chapter is really about *being the gift*. YOU are the gift. It may not seem like it, but you definitely are a gift. If you are willing and available, there are many ways that God can use you as a gift to someone else. It's up to you to prepare yourself to be that gift.

In order to prepare, you must first make your heart free of judgment and condemnation toward others as best you can. You will never be perfect, but you can always strive to become better. You should be able to identify when your personal feelings are getting in the way of you being presented as a gift to someone. In that situation, the responsible and compassionate thing to do is to gracefully remove yourself from the situation. Get out of the way and God can use someone else who is better prepared for the job. But, if you find yourself missing a chance to be a gift because you weren't ready, don't miss the opportunity to work on that part of yourself. The opportunity was brought to your attention for a reason. Don't ever miss the lesson. It has come to help you grow.

Once you have made yourself available, try to become open to opportunities to give. You will not have to look very hard to see them. Opportunities to give are all around you. They present themselves to you daily. You just have to be present and pay attention. Make it your intention to be helpful to other human beings and it will happen. In most instances, your giving will come so naturally that you may not realize that you just blessed someone. This is because when your heart is pure and your desire is to give just for the sake of giving, it becomes just another thing in your day that made you smile. When you are at the store and you hold the door for the next person, you may not feel like you did anything at all. But you could have made that person's day with a small act of kindness and a smile. You may not even know when you have given a gift to someone because it doesn't deplete you in any way. Let me share a story from a friend.

A close friend of mine shared this story with me. Like me in the early 2000's, she was also in tough financial circumstances. We were literally making it from day to day. She told me she stopped for gas one morning on the way to the office and as she waited for the attendant to pump her gas, her eyes met with a woman.

The woman was sitting in another car waiting for the attendant and she looked upset. My friend smiled and said, "Good morning." The woman returned the salutation and then drove away when her transaction was done. When my friend presented payment to the attendant for her gas, he informed her that her gas already been paid for by the woman in the other car. Somehow, by saying Good Morning, she had given that woman something so special that she was moved to try to reciprocate in some way. Experiences like these are always amazing and make you think.

It is very likely that my friend was putting her last few dollars into her gas tank that morning and had no idea how she would buy more gas when that ran out. But aside from her circumstances, she still had a valuable gift to give, "Good morning" and a smile. It didn't cost her anything, but it meant the world to someone else. Do you see how you are always able to be a gift if you make yourself available? And once you make it your intention, it becomes so normal that you may not always realize when you are blessing someone. You just become a blessing and by blessing others, you are blessed. By giving to others, you receive gifts. Not because that is your motivation or expectation, it is the law of giving.

By giving, you receive, and by blessing, you are blessed. My friend received an instant gift right back that morning. Sometimes it happens that way and you can notice it. But it can also be more long term like my story about my house or about my music. Either way, this spiritual law never fails.

To sum up verses 38 and 39, we should first approach others with forgiveness and understanding. Then you will receive forgiveness and understanding from God and others because those are the seeds that you have sown. In this scenario, there is no room for us to judge and criticize those who we have been chosen to help, unless judgment and criticism is what we wish to receive.

When you are limitless in the love, forgiveness, and understanding you show toward others, the love, forgiveness, and understanding you receive will also be limitless. But if you are restrained in how far you will go in loving, forgiving, and understanding others, you will receive these kindnesses from others with the same amount of restraint. You receive what you give by the same measure, large or small.

So understand that you have the power to invoke unlimited blessings upon your own life through the way you serve others. When you give time, you will always have enough time. When you give love, you will always have enough love. Do you give money? Then you will always have enough money. Give food and you'll be blessed with more food. Give laughter and you'll be blessed with laughter. I give music. I know I will always have enough music and since music is my love, there is no greater reward for me.

This well known prayer by Saint Frances of Assisi is one of my favorite. It puts this whole concept of being the gift into perfect perspective. Let us focus on being the gift and our lives will always be blessed even through our own challenges and struggles.

*Lord, make me an instrument of Thy peace;*
*where there is hatred, let me sow love;*
*where there is injury, pardon;*
*where there is doubt, faith;*
*where there is despair, hope;*
*where there is darkness, light;*
*and where there is sadness, joy.*

*O Divine Master,*
*grant that I may not so much seek to be consoled as to*
*console;*
*to be understood, as to understand;*
*to be loved, as to love;*
*for it is in giving that we receive,*
*it is in pardoning that we are pardoned,*
*and it is in dying that we are born to eternal life.*

*Amen.*

*Francis of Assisi*

## CHAPTER TEN: MEETING THE CHALLENGE

Luke 6:39-40

*39  He further told them a proverb: Can a blind [man]
guide and direct a blind [man]? Will they not both
stumble into a ditch or a hole in the ground?*
*40  A pupil is not superior to his teacher, but everyone
[when he is] completely trained (readjusted, restored,
set to rights, and perfected) will be like his teacher.*

Often, the friends and people with whom we
associate tend to lack the same things. Like attracts
like. We often feel more comfortable around people
who have the same struggles as we do. When I was in
a troubled marriage, my closest confidants were also in
troubled relationships. We complained about our
husbands to each other over lunch on Wednesdays
and we were comfortable doing so, because we all
had similar challenges. We felt safe discussing the

mistreatment that we suffered because we knew no one would think less of us because of it. Our little circle of friends was a safe zone where we were not judged. We talked to each other, hung out together and served as each other's hotline in a marital crisis. We often came to each other's aid and helped when we could. We all had young children. So it was easy to band together and support each other emotionally and spiritually. We attended church together, prayed for one another, and it was a good and comfortable thing to spend time around someone who understood what we were all going through. However, as I said, we all lacked some of the same things.

So here's the question. Can the blind actually lead the blind? Don't we both risk fall into a ditch together? We can support and empathize with each other. We can be a shoulder to cry on. But how can we provide something that we lack? The support between my friends and me had been comforting, but understandably limited since we had a lot of the same problems. This continued right through our divorces and the years following as single mothers raising our children.

We often pooled our resources and made the best of difficult situations. Although we had similar struggles in our personal lives, we were all unique and that is also what drew us together as friends. That's what we had to offer each other. It is not only what you have in common, but uniqueness is often what draws you together with other human beings.

You are chosen for specific tasks and services because of what is in you – the things God has placed in you through birth and life experiences up to this point. God needs to impart to others that which He has placed in you. He can't use someone else for your job, because you are one-of-a-kind. When He created you, he broke the mold and there's not another human being (past, present, or future) who is exactly like you. Isn't that the most amazing thing? Billions of people have passed through their journeys on this planet and not two of them are exactly the same. This should tell you that when God places an opportunity in front of you, it is for YOU specifically.

No one else has exactly your DNA, your temperament, your perspective, and your heart. When you notice something, there is a reason. You are the special person who is equipped for that task. When you notice a person that needs your gifts, it is because no one else can present those gifts quite like you and you are perfect for the job. Our prayer should be to always show up where we're supposed to be and to notice the things we are supposed to see so we don't miss the precious opportunity to be a gift to someone who needs us.

People need you. It might be a foreign thought at first, maybe even uncomfortable. People need your gifts and your talents to improve their lives. Verse 39 asks the question, "Can a blind man lead a blind man?" Think about it. If you and I have the same exact needs, how much can we help each other? If we both lack the same things, how much can we give to each other? A problem is drawn to its solution. If a problem presents itself to you, it's because you are the solution. You have the missing part and you have an abundance of what is lacking there. For friendship, we are drawn together by our sameness. But in this concept, you are drawn to others because of your differences. Like a magnetic force, opposites are drawn together.

So here's what's so exciting about this concept. Many people you encounter on your journey need something that you have. But, you also need something from them. When I opened my home to people who needed a place to stay, I didn't feel like I needed anything from them. My intention was to help ease their difficulties, not to gain anything for myself. But in return, I received a lot. Each one of them added to our lives. There were good times in our house. Whether it was shared mealtimes, cookouts in the backyard, movie nights, family outings, or just funny conversations, the people we helped also helped us. My children and I have fond memories of everyone who ever lived in our house with us because they added something positive to our lives.

So, yes, you are special and unique. You are chosen to help people who really need you. Otherwise, none of this would make any sense. But, you also gain from the experience in some way. I believe God made it this way because we need to always remember that no one is better than anyone else. You may have more resources, education, time, etc. No matter what we have accomplished and accumulated in life, we are all still the same in God's eyes. Remembering this allows us to approach one another in humility and gentleness; interacting with a spirit of kindness and patience with the shortcomings of others and reminds us that we are not perfect. No one is.

But this goes even deeper. Have you ever been talking to someone and found yourself sounding exactly like your mom or like a mentor of yours? Maybe when you are in the middle of a task you hear your dad's voice in your head telling you what to do next. Or how many times has your child started a sentence with the words, "My teacher said..."? This is because each time you make yourself a gift to someone by helping them in some way, you deposit a little bit of yourself into them, like a teacher. By impacting someone's life, you plant a seed in them and as it grows, they become a little more like you in some way. That seed is a little bit of you and it grows to become a new skill, ability, source of strength, or area of knowledge that will help that person become more capable or fulfilled in an area where they were once lacking.

Verse 40 tells us that everyone who is well taught will be like his teacher. Everyone who you have effectively helped in some way, even if you just had an encouraging conversation with them, will be a little more like you in that way. From your encouragement, they might be better able to encourage someone else. From your smile, they might be more inclined to offer a smile to others. Because you held the door for them, they might remember to hold a door for someone else. Your kindness is a seed that you plant for the sake of planting. You saw a good spot for it and you planted it. It is not necessarily your job to go back and water that seed or watch it grow. You

You have added some good to the world.

are only the planter. It will be up to that person what happens to it after that. But you can have faith that your positive actions when properly guided and performed will always yield a positive effect on that person. It will serve as a starting point to something wonderful in his or her life. It will also spread to touch those around them and beyond.  This is an amazing spiritual concept.

Just imagine that you plant a flower seed in a place that you thought could use some sprucing up. Then the rain and the sun nurture the seed's growth into a full flower.  The bees come along to pollinate it as the wind blows its seeds to the surrounding area. That flower becomes like you in that it spreads more seeds. Then those seeds are planted and go through the same process.  How long would it be before your one seed brings about a field of flowers?  If you never came back to see the field of flowers, your seed will still have been the one that started it all.  The laws of nature will take your seed and make it more than you could imagine.  God's spiritual laws will take your gift and make it more than you can ever dream.  And even if you never see it, you will have been the starting point for something truly magnificent.  You will have added some love and positivity to the world.  So each time you are able to sow into someone else's life, however small and seemingly insignificant, you can move on from that point knowing that you have added some good to the world and that has the potential to grow.

So we come together with people in friendship because of what we have in common. Similar tastes and interests bond us together and make for a fulfilling relationship. Even in friendship, our differences serve to enhance each other in positive ways. Real friends inspire personal growth and make each other better. However, people are also drawn together because of their differences. When you need something, you are naturally drawn toward that thing and when you have something, you are drawn to that need. Our challenge is to be available to meet a need when we become aware of it. Just know that when you fulfill a need for someone else, there's always a surprise in it for you! Somehow, you always receive in the giving, but giving should be your sole objective.

## CHAPTER ELEVEN: TAKE A LOOK IN THE MIRROR

Luke 6:41-45

*41 Why do you see the speck that is in your brother's eye but do not notice or consider the beam [of timber] that is in your own eye?*

*42 Or how can you say to your brother, Brother, allow me to take out the speck that is in your eye, when you yourself do not see the beam that is in your own eye? You actor (pretender, hypocrite)! First take the beam out of your own eye, and then you will see clearly to take out the speck that is in your brother's eye.*

*43 For there is no good (healthy) tree that bears decayed (worthless, stale) fruit, nor on the other hand does a decayed (worthless, sickly) tree bear good fruit.*

*44 For each tree is known and identified by its own fruit; for figs are not gathered from thornbushes, nor is a cluster of grapes picked from a bramblebush.*

*45 The upright (honorable, intrinsically good) man out of the good treasure [stored] in his heart produces what is upright (honorable and intrinsically good), and the evil man out of the evil storehouse brings forth that which is depraved (wicked and intrinsically evil); for out of the abundance (overflow) of the heart his mouth speaks.*

Why would you spend your time and energy pointing out the shortcomings of someone else while not identifying areas in your own life that are in need of correction? How can you attempt to correct another person's flaws when you haven't yet worked on your own? This kind of carelessness will make you less effective in the good things that you attempt to do for others. It's like the nice volunteer at the free clinic who insulted me so terribly without even realizing it. I will never forget her. She is burned into my memory not because of the good work she was doing, but because of her own lack of compassion and courtesy. It is necessary for you to always look to identify areas for growth and improvement in your own life. As you learn and grow, you become better suited to be helpful to someone else. You become more prepared and effective to be a blessing. Blessings should not come with a bitter taste. They should be sweet and soothing to the person who receives them. It should be a divine comfort in difficult times. With this in mind, we must be ever so careful to always endeavor to prepare ourselves for service -- to become better and more useful to our fellow man. Our job is to love and take care of each other and to do it with all goodness, kindness and compassion.

*"By this shall all [men] know that you are My disciples, if you love one another [if you keep on showing love among yourselves]." ~ John 13:35*

This all boils down to what's on the inside. What you do depends on what is in your heart. It really doesn't matter what you try to portray on the outside. What is inside of you will show on the outside, even when you are unaware of it. I believe the woman at the clinic was trying to do good by volunteering her time and skills to help the less fortunate. I believe her intentions were good. But I also believe that in her heart, she looked down upon those poor people who needed that clinic. I don't pretend to know why, but I really think that she despised us in her heart. Let me qualify this thought by saying that I may not be the most objective person to make this observation. I admit that I could have been overly sensitive because of my circumstances. Nevertheless, I think she had some things in her heart that needed work. That's my observation.

Many times, we may try to put our personal feelings aside in a situation. We may try to do some things in spite of the way we feel. I believe such decisions are mostly well intended, but here's the problem. We can't "put feelings aside" and go on with life. Feelings are important. If there is something that needs to be put aside then that means it's getting in the way. If it's getting in the way then it is something that shouldn't be there at all. Don't put it aside. Deal with it. It's trying to tell you something. Put it right in front of you and take a good look at it. Ask it questions. Find out why and how it got there. Figure out how long it has been there. See what it needs to teach you. Then you can move on without it ever bothering you again.

> What is inside of you will show on the outside.

When you feel judgmental toward someone and you *put it aside*, you actually *bury it inside*. It gets in the way. It's not pretty to look at. So you shove it down someplace where you can no longer see it and then you try to forget about it. But, it continues to exist even if you never look at it, even if you manage to forget about it. Our brains are very powerful. You can really convince yourself of anything and if you try hard enough, it will become your reality. So when you hide that negative feeling and try to convince yourself that it's not there. You may very well forget about it. The problem is that until you deal with it, it will still be there and it will still have an effect on you.

Verses 43-45 tell us that what is inside of you will show on the outside. Something cannot come out of you that isn't inside of you. You will not display resentful behavior toward someone unless you have resentment. You will not be an angry person unless there is anger on the inside. A tree is known by the fruit it bears. You may work very hard to keep it under wraps but what is inside of you will seep out through the cracks when you least expect it. At an emotional time, it will bubble over and make a mess. It cannot stay neatly where you hide it. It will produce *fruit* and that fruit is also a teacher. If you do not ignore it, it will teach you about yourself and help you grow.

Can you think of someone you know who always seems angry? You may not be quite sure what they are angry about at any given moment, but you can feel the angry energy when you are around them. I have observed people who are like this and at times, I have seen it in myself. It's interesting to watch. An angry person doesn't always appear angry on the outside. When someone carries something, like anger or sadness, they can become quite skilled at masking it when they don't want it to be seen by others.

I have observed a parent in public with children who can be pleasant to other people around them and in an instant become unkind toward their child. It's amazing. I have seen a person who seems happy and then becomes violent because of a minor disagreement. I'm sure they don't even realize they are behaving is such a contradictory manner. The fact is that they are angry, frustrated or overwhelmed in some way, but they are holding it in, in order to interact appropriately in public. However, when relationships are intimate, like with parents and children, or situations become stressful like a disagreement, it can be difficult to mask hidden emotions. It's like a pressure cooker and when it comes out, it's usually more intense than expected.

You have heard the term "bottled up emotions". What happens when something is bottled up and under pressure? Eventually, it explodes. Or even when there is no explosion, little bits occasionally seep out to relieve the building pressure. There are always signs of what's going on inside, no matter how well someone thinks they are hiding their true feelings. That is why it is not wise to try to stuff down the negativity that we experience in our lives.

Even our negative experiences are here to teach us and to help us grow. If we open ourselves to the experience and the lesson, although it may be difficult, we will eventually be able to move through the experience instead of being stuck in it. We may experience hurt, loss, illness, sadness, anger, overwhelm, or despair. There are real challenges in this human journey that are unavoidable. Life will often bring you situations that you never imagined you would face. But, the fact that it has become a part of your journey means that you have what it takes to meet the challenge, learn from it, and move on. Don't run from it, don't hide from it, don't be embarrassed by it, and don't get stuck in the struggle. It's all a part of life and that experience is now a part of you.

We are all human. We all have flaws. But, our flaws are also a part of us. There is no part of you that isn't important and deserving of your love and attention, even the negative parts. Everything in life is a part of the balance; the equilibrium of living this human experience. There is good and bad, right and wrong, up and down. One cannot exist without the other. So your weaknesses are as important as your strengths. Without weakness you couldn't know strength. Without pain you couldn't know pleasure. There's no satiety without hunger. Instead of trying to avoid the parts of us that we see as dark or negative, we must value them equally as we do our positive traits and our strengths. Our weaknesses, struggles, and flaws are here to teach us important lessons and to guide us to our best selves. So when you recognize a part of yourself that you are not proud of, don't hide it or ignore it. Bring it out into the light. Take a good look at it and ask it some questions. See what it is showing you. Hear what it is telling you. Endeavor to learn the lesson and then be grateful for it. Say thank you and when the lesson is learned, that thing will no longer need your attention.

So when one of these teachers shows up in your life, be receptive to it and willing to learn. Don't bother with shame, embarrassment, or guilt. Remind yourself that you are human and you have things to work on. Then give yourself permission to learn and grow. The fact that you are recognizing the teacher means that you are ready for the lesson. It is the right time and you are prepared, even if you think you're not. Trust yourself to understand and recognize what needs to be done. Then do it. You will be rewarded with personal growth and the result will be a better you.

Here's another piece to the puzzle. We all have things about others that drive us nuts. You know the things that get under your skin; the nails on the chalkboard. Do you ever wonder why some people's personality or behavior could bother you so much? Why do you care? Why can't you just ignore it? The reason is because that one thing that really gets your goat is also a part of you. That is why you are so familiar with it and it can have such an effect on you. It took me a while to grasp this concept mainly because I don't think we want to believe that the thing that we despise also exists in us. But it does.

Pay attention because this is just one way that life will show you to yourself. It's like a mirror. When something about someone else grabs your attention and causes a strong reaction within you, that's your mirror. Look long and hard. Your slip might be hanging or there's spinach in your teach. As humans, we have the tendency to try conceal the things that we don't like about ourselves. First, so we don't have to look at it and second, so others won't know about it. But, as I stated earlier, what's on the inside will show on the outside, even when you don't know it is showing. And the funny thing is, others can usually see it when you cannot.

When you see something that you find to be blatantly offensive in others, look closely. It is likely that you are looking at a mirror. So pay close attention to what is being shown to you. Then ask why, because there is a lesson to be learned. Don't judge yourself or the other person. Thank the teacher for showing up and blessing you with the lesson that will eventually lead to a better you. This is one more way that life directs us toward personal growth. Ultimately, living is about growth. Anything that doesn't grow and change is not alive.

*"For there is nothing hidden that shall not be disclosed, nor anything secret that shall not be known and come out into the open." ~Luke 8:17*

The bottom line is there's no faking it; no keeping of outer appearances. All things will come to light. What's on the inside of you is the real you. So you should always be cognizant of what is truly in your heart, both the good and not-so-good. There's no judgment, only lessons to be learned.

Being the most authentic version of you is the best thing you can do to help someone else. Accepting and loving yourself wholly will enable you to accept and love others. Then your actions will be more closely aligned with your intentions. Self-exploration, learning, and growing means you are truly alive.

## CHAPTER TWELVE: OBEDIENCE EQUALS REWARDS

Luke 6:46-49

46  *And why call ye me, Lord, Lord, and do not the things which I say?*

47  *Every one that cometh unto me, and heareth my words, and doeth them, I will show you to whom he is like:*

48  *he is like a man building a house, who digged and went deep, and laid a foundation upon the rock: and when a flood arose, the stream brake against that house, and could not shake it: because it had been well builded.*

49  *But he that heareth, and doeth not, is like a man that built a house upon the earth without a foundation; against which the stream brake, and straightway it fell in; and the ruin of that house was great.*

Imagine you had a personal visit from Jesus, himself. One morning there's a knock on the door and there he is. He tells you that he has some information for you and instead of texting you, he decided to stop by. He says there are some questions he would like to answer in order to help you along your life's journey and asks you if you have time. Of course you graciously accept this unexpected visitor as you anticipate this will be a spectacular day. You have been selected for a personal sit-down with the master teacher. You feel like you won the lottery and you put on water for tea.

Jesus starts out by explaining that he knows you have some questions about your life's purpose and are wondering if you are fulfilling whatever it might be. You are unsure why you are here. So he begins by telling you that you don't have to concern yourself with what others think of you. You should only endeavor to know your authentic self and to seek to know the God who created you. By doing this you will find the answers.

*"But seek (aim at and strive after) first of all His kingdom and His righteousness (His way of doing and being right), and then all these things taken together will be given you besides." ~Matthew 6:33*

Jesus goes on to say that he chose to come to your house today because you are ready to hear the things he's about to tell you. He says you are ready to understand and use this information. And so your chat begins a pleasant day of listening, asking questions, and taking lots of notes. You are thrilled at the opportunity to learn at the feet of the master and to gain from his wisdom. After a few hours, your lesson is drawing to a close. You are full with the whole experience and basking in the blessing of it all. What a privilege!

### What's the point?

This is all so wonderful but what, exactly, is the point of it all? What have you gained by reading this book? Hopefully, you have gained a better understanding of yourself and your purpose for being here. You have found direction for your personal growth. That is the point of it all, to help you grow, to help you find purpose, to tell you that we are all connected and you matter in this world.

## What have you learned about yourself?

I hope by reading this you have learned something about yourself and how valuable you are. You are uniquely created for a specific purpose that only you can fulfill in your own way. Your experiences in life are yours alone and they have prepared you in way that is not the same as any other human being on earth, past, present, or future. People can be very much alike, but even identical twins are distinguishable from one another. God only created one you and then He broke the proverbial mold. You are the only YOU there is and that is awesome. No one can ever be a better YOU!

You are the answer to a question; the solution to a problem. Inside of you is the voice of inspiration that will guide you. If you can believe that God has already given you everything you need at this moment and you can trust that voice of inspiration inside of you, then you are ready to walk in your purpose. You are ready to discover new and creative ways to serve your fellowman. You are prepared to turn your compassion into action in the service of mankind.

You can now realize that living your purpose may not always seem like an extraordinary gesture. It may often appear as small, seemingly insignificant acts of kindness that you are inspired to make toward another person. It may appear as a warm feeling inside after you exchange a smile with a stranger or pass someone a tissue. Living your purpose is distinctively your experience and will not be duplicated by another person.

### What will you do with what you have learned?

Gaining this new understanding of yourself and your purpose is a great gift to you. So what will you do with this gift? In verse 46, Jesus asks why would you to revere him highly and not follow his advice. That wouldn't make sense, would it? Would you be so happy and blessed by that personal visit from the Master Teacher and then do nothing that he taught you? Would you just go back to your daily life without making any effort to incorporate this new knowledge into it? That would be like getting the most valuable, beautiful gift from someone and just putting it in the closet to collect dust. Then what is its real value?

What is the value of what you have learned by reading this book? What is the point of learning this and not applying it to your own life? It's like winning a beautiful, new dream house and refusing to live in it. You're probably saying, "I'd never do that!" But, will you? If you can't comprehend the value of a thing, you might not be able to really appreciate its power to change your life.

## What is the value in learning these things?

Remember the mother in the documentary who, after all of her hard work and diligence, was about to be approved for a brand new house for her family? But, at the eleventh hour she waivered and abandoned her blessing. We can never be sure exactly why she did it, but she chose not to take advantage of a great gift to her life. From our perspective on the outside looking in, we can't understand why she couldn't comprehend the value in that opportunity. Why didn't she want to improve her situation? We don't know. But take a lesson from her story. Don't be the person who reads this book, learns valuable insights to enhance your growth toward your own life's purpose, and then walk away from what you have learned.

Jesus, in Verse 49, said such a decision is not well thought out. It is like a builder who, instead of laying a proper foundation, builds a beautiful house on the sand. So when the storm came and the waters rose, the house could not withstand and it was immediately destroyed. What was the value in that beautiful new home? It was nothing. It was a beautiful thing with a lot of potential, but the actions of the builder rendered it worthless. No matter how much you learned by reading this book, if you fail to apply it to your life, it is worthless.

But, to the person who takes these lessons and immediately endeavors to apply them to his or her own life, this little book is priceless. It can be the starting point to launch your life into new and positive directions. Verse 48 says if you are that person, you are like a builder with a great plan, who digs down to the rock and lays a sure and stable foundation on which to build a beautiful house. Then when the storms came, the house was unshakeable. It was strong enough to withstand the wind and the flood. What is the value of that builder's house?

## *Which one are you?*

Which builder are you? Anyone can pick up a book and read it. Anyone can attend a lecture, log in to a webinar, or watch a TV show. There are many ways to learn new things. The lessons are all around you. But in order to become more enlightened, you must be willing to apply what you learn to your everyday life. You have to be willing to step out of your comfort zone and in some small way, DO what you have learned. Only then will you begin to expand your consciousness and see how amazing you really are. You can't expect things to change until you start changing things. It might seem strange and uncomfortable at first. But, trust me when I say, "YOU CAN DO IT!" Trust yourself. Let go of your fear and trust God.

*"Our deepest fear is not that we are inadequate. Our deepest fear is that we are powerful beyond measure."*

*– From A Return to Love by Marianne Williamson*

## CONCLUSION: WILL YOU ACCEPT THE CALL

This is the operator. Will you accept this call? God is calling us all to a higher place. It is a necessary challenge with potential for great rewards. If you are obedient to the call, it will lead you to where you want to be; more peace, more fulfillment, more gratitude in your life.

You can experience fulfillment and a more peaceful life by seeking to identify the gifts God has placed in you to be shared with mankind. For some of us, our gifts are very apparent. For others, we have yet to begin to identify our gifts. But rest assured that we all are endowed with wonderful treasures with the sole purpose of serving and enriching the lives of your fellowman.

So what will you do? How will you begin? Now that you have this information, you can no longer say that you don't know. Here's where you begin...

1. **The Final Authority** – Realizing that there is one God who created us all, get to know your creator. Understand that God has sent you on this journey for a reason. *Look to Him to find your purpose.*

2. **Accepting the Call** – Everyone is called to contribute to this earthly experience in a positive way. We all came here from the same source. So we are one family. By your desire to grow in the direction of your destiny, choose to accept the call. Many people go through life as if they are asleep, going from day to day in a routine without noticing all the connections between us. *Wake up and accept the call to a higher place.*

3. **The Chosen Few** – When there is a call for volunteers for something, everyone is called. However, everyone is not chosen. The ones who step forward and offer themselves for a task are chosen for it. The majority of people

will not be chosen. Because they will not step forward.

> *For many are called (invited and summoned), but few are chosen. ~Matthew 22:14*

You are ready to make a positive contribution to this world. <u>Step forward and be chosen.</u>

4. **You are the Solution** – You have the answer to somebody's need or problem. You have an abundance of what someone else lacks. Since problems are drawn toward a solution, people who need you are all around you. Just pay attention. Helping them will not deplete you in any way. It will only add to your own blessings.

> *The blessing of the Lord—it makes [truly] rich, and He adds no sorrow with it [neither does toiling increase it]. ~Proverbs 10:22*

Now that you know you are the solution, <u>BE the solution.</u>

5. **For the Least of These** – Now you know that everything that has happened in your life was

for a reason. Although you may not know the reasons, you have to trust that all of your life experiences have helped to make you who you are today. Those experiences have uniquely equipped you with certain understanding and abilities. If you submit, God will use all of those experiences for your good.

Now let it go. Do not hold on to negativity. Forgive others who wronged you and forgive yourself for your mistakes. It was all a part of the plan. *Always remember that God is with you.*

*As for you, you thought evil against me, but God meant it for good, to bring about that many people should be kept alive, as they are this day.*

*~ Genesis 50:20*

6. **It's Not About You** – You are blessed in order to be a blessing to others. It is a continuous flow that envelops us all. You receive so that you can give. Then in giving you continue to receive. If you want more, give more. Notice

the things you have in abundance; things of which you have more than you need. *Then give freely to those who are in need.*

7. **Who Needs You** – It's time to stop seeing others as different from you and to notice the sameness. We are all one race, human, and one species. We all originated from the same source and we need each other. When you consider another person, think of your connection to them, not the perceived distance between you. Know that all people deserve your consideration and respect. You don't have to understand why they are the way they are. Just accept that they are human like you and treat people they way you want to be treated.

8. **Paying Forward** – The reason for paying forward is not to make you feel good. It is a way for you to add some kindness and positivity to the world. So as you begin practicing how to share your gifts with others, be careful not to take anything away. Try to empathize and see things from the other

person's point of view. Be mindful, discrete, and kind. No matter what you are giving, remember to do your best not to belittle, insult, or embarrass the person you want to help. Whenever you give, <u>help them to also receive a measure of dignity, hope, self-worth, and success.</u>

9. **Giving Back** – You know now that you have been blessed in order to be a blessing to someone else. When you give what you have to help another, you invoke the law of sowing and reaping in your own life. If you sow love, you will receive more love. When you sow kindness, more kindness will be shown to you. Whatever you give, you will find that it will be returned to you in some way and you will never run out of it. When you are inspired to give, don't worry about decreasing what you have. You have been blessed with more than enough so that you can share with someone else. <u>Share freely knowing that you will be blessed with more.</u>

10. **Meeting The Challenge** – You are special with a unique set of experiences and abilities. When God chooses you for a job, please know that no one can do it quite like you can. What you have to offer the world is important. Don't compare yourself to others. Just be you. <u>Be your best self, because nobody can be a better you than you can.</u>

11. **Take a Look in the Mirror** – Self examination is always healthy and necessary. Seek to know yourself completely. Don't reject or hide parts of yourself that you think are negative or undesirable. All of the parts of you are important. Love yourself. Care for yourself. Forgive yourself. Of all the things that you gladly offer to others through your kindness, you are also worthy. <u>You are enough and worthy of love.</u>

12. **Obedience Equals Reward** – All that you have learned here is of little value unless you put it to practical use. Now that you understand how you can begin to grow in the direction of your life's purpose, you have to make a

move. You have to DO something. It doesn't have to be a grand gesture. <u>Begin with the smallest step outside of your comfort zone and you will be on your way!</u>

It is said that you cannot see something until you are ready and willing to see it. If you have read this book and understood its concepts, then you are ready. You understand what you have to do and you are prepared to do it. It is quite likely that you have already been practicing all of these concepts. You didn't have a label for it. You just followed your inner leading.

Now you have a framework on which to build a more deliberate approach to using your gifts in service of other people. You can intentionally participate in the laws of giving and receiving. You can purposefully improve and enrich the lives of others while fulfilling your own destiny. I say, you are ready to wake up and be the good that you seek to find in the world.

Be the person you wish all others to be. Sow your seeds in the fertile ground of people and believe that your goodness will be multiplied over and over again. Be the mirror that shows them the good that lies within them. Smile at your neighbor. Hold a door. Take time to listen and you will be inspired in new ways. You will be amazed at how this new attitude, this renewing of your mind, will bless your life as well as those around you. Do it for your highest good and the highest good of everyone involved. Godspeed, my friend, peace be the journey!

## Musical Suggestions

Because I am a musical person, there is a soundtrack that plays in my head most of the time. It is comprised of all the different genres of music that I listen to. As I am inspired to write on different subjects, along with the words comes music for the soundtrack. So here are my musical suggestions for this book.

Use these few songs to start your inspirational playlist. Look them up and listen to them. Pay close attention to the lyrics. The messages in these songs might inspire you as you begin your new endeavor. Add on more suggestions of your own as they come to you. Then share them with someone.

♫ *Shower the People*, James Taylor, Warner Bros. 1976

♫ *Man in the Mirror*, Michael Jackson, Epic/Sony Legacy 1987

♫ *Because You Loved Me*, Celine Dion, Columbia 1996

♫ *I Need You to Survive*, Hezekiah Walker & The Love Fellowship Choir, Verity 2002

♫ *One*, India Arie, Motown Records 2013

♫ *We Are Here*, Alicia Keys, RCA Records 2014

♫ _____

_____

♫ _____

_____

♫ _____

_____

♫ _____

_____

♫ _____

_____

♫ _____

_____

*Namasté*

*(nah-mas-tay)*

*My soul honors your soul.*
*I honor the place in you where*
*the entire universe resides.*
*I honor the light, love, truth,*
*beauty, and peace within you,*
*because it is also within me.*
*In sharing these things,*
*we are united, we are the same,*
*we are one.*

[An ancient Hindu greeting]

The Lord bless you and watch, guard, and keep you;

The Lord make His face to shine upon and enlighten you and be gracious (kind, merciful, and giving favor) to you;

The Lord lift up His [approving] countenance upon you and give you peace (tranquility of heart and life continually).

~Numbers 6:24-26

## About the Author

Deborah A. Vaughn is a mother of three children, currently living in New Jersey. She received a Bachelors Degree in Computer Science from Kean University and a Masters of Communication and Information Studies from Rutgers University both in New Jersey. She is a NJ Certified teacher and a professional singer/actress. She has performed in musical theater, choirs, cover bands, and concerts throughout New Jersey and has toured internationally as a singer. Biblical study is the foundation through which her many interests and talents have grown. She has a love for learning, spirituality, children, music and the arts.

Made in the USA
Charleston, SC
29 December 2014